Cambridge Certificate in Advanced English 2

WITH ANSWERS

Official examination papers from University of Cambridge ESOL Examinations

CAMBRIDGE UNIVERSITY PRESS
Cambridge, New York, Melbourne, Madrid, Cape Town, Singapore, São Paulo, Delhi

Cambridge University Press
The Edinburgh Building, Cambridge CB2 8RU, UK

www.cambridge.org
Information on this title: www.cambridge.org/9780521714471

© Cambridge University Press 2008

It is normally necessary for written permission for copying to be obtained in advance from a publisher. The candidate answer sheets at the back of this book are designed to be copied and distributed in class. The normal requirements are waived here and it is not necessary to write to Cambridge University Press for permission for an individual teacher to make copies for use within his or her own classroom. Only those pages which carry the wording '© UCLES 2008 Photocopiable' may be copied.

First published 2008

Printed in the United Kingdom at the University Press, Cambridge

A catalogue record for this publication is available from the British Library

ISBN 978-0-521-714464   Student's Book without answers

ISBN 978-0-521-714471   Student's Book with answers

ISBN 978-0-521-714495   Audio CD Set

ISBN 978-0-521-714488   Self-study Pack

Contents

Thanks and acknowledgements   *4*

Introduction   *5*

Test 1	Paper 1	Reading	*7*
	Paper 2	Writing	*16*
	Paper 3	Use of English	*18*
	Paper 4	Listening	*26*
	Paper 5	Speaking	*31*

Test 2	Paper 1	Reading	*33*
	Paper 2	Writing	*42*
	Paper 3	Use of English	*44*
	Paper 4	Listening	*52*
	Paper 5	Speaking	*57*

Test 3	Paper 1	Reading	*59*
	Paper 2	Writing	*68*
	Paper 3	Use of English	*70*
	Paper 4	Listening	*78*
	Paper 5	Speaking	*83*

Test 4	Paper 1	Reading	*85*
	Paper 2	Writing	*94*
	Paper 3	Use of English	*96*
	Paper 4	Listening	*104*
	Paper 5	Speaking	*109*

Visual materials for Paper 5   *colour section*

Test 1	Paper 5 frames	*110*
Test 2	Paper 5 frames	*113*
Test 3	Paper 5 frames	*116*
Test 4	Paper 5 frames	*119*

Marks and results   *122*

Test 1	Key and transcript	*133*
Test 2	Key and transcript	*144*
Test 3	Key and transcript	*155*
Test 4	Key and transcript	*166*

Sample answer sheets   *177*

Thanks and acknowledgements

The authors and publishers acknowledge the following sources of copyright material and are grateful for the permissions granted. While every effort has been made, it has not always been possible to identify the sources of all the material used, or to trace all copyright holders. If any omissions are brought to our notice, we will be happy to include the appropriate acknowledgements on reprinting.

The Telegraph Media Group Limited for the adapted text on p. 7 'Extract from a Book Review, The Snow Geese' by Edward Smith, *Sunday Telegraph* 24 March 2002, for the adapted text on p. 8 'Tools' by Jeff Howell, *Sunday Telegraph* 23 December 2001, for the text on p. 67 'Do reviews sell books?' *Sunday Telegraph* 1 January 1995, for the text on p. 90 'The Hotel Inspector' from 'A night with the avenging angel' by Christopher Middleton, *Daily Telegraph* 18 April 1996. Copyright © The Telegraph Media Group Limited; Financial Times for the adapted text on p. 9 'Book Crossing' from 'The flutter of tiny pages in the wild' by Margaret McCartney, *Financial Times Weekend* 8 May 2004, for the adapted text on p. 21 'Snow-kiting: an alternative form of skiing?' from 'Snow Future' *Financial Times Weekend* 30 December 2000. Copyright © Financial Times Limited; Classic FM Magazine for the text on pp. 10–11 'The Magic Lute' by Chris Wilson, *Classic FM Magazine* 16 June 1996. Reproduced by permission of Classic FM Magazine: The Directory of Social Change for the text on p. 15 'Organising local events' by Sarah Passingham. *Organising Local Events*. Copyright © 1993. Reproduced by kind permission of the publishers, The Directory of Social Change, 24 Stephenson Way, London NW1 2DP, tel: 08450 77 77 07, from whom copies may be purchased; The Guardian for the adapted text on p. 35 'The Happiest Country' from 'Vanuatu tops wellbeing and environment index' by Duncan Campbell, *The Guardian* 12 July 2006. Copyright © Guardian News and Media Ltd 2006; NI Syndication Limited for the adapted text on p. 46 'Traffic Jams are nothing new' from 'Case of Jam Today and Jam Yesterday' by Kevin Eason, *The Times* 8 June 1996. Reproduced by permission of NI Syndication Limited 1996; Penguin Books Ltd and Sagalyn Agency for the adapted text on p. 59 'Decision making in business: Gordon Bethune', Excerpted from *Lessons from the Top: 50 Most Successful Business Leaders in America – and What You Can Learn From Them*. Copyright © Thomas Neff and James Citrin, 1999, 2001 (Penguin, Currency/Doubleday). All Rights Reserved. Reproduced by permission of Penguin Books Ltd and Sagalyn Agency; The Society of Authors for the extract on p. 60 'Children's toys' from *The Shrimp and the Anemone* by L P Hartley. Reproduced by permission of the Society of Authors as the Literary Representative of the Estate of L P Hartley; Energize Website Library for the adapted text on p. 61 'Children's involvement in family decision making' from *Leading Small Groups* by Nathan W Turner, Judson Press, 1996. Found in the Energize website library at: http://www.energizeinc.com/art.html; Charles Clover for the article on p. 64 'Solar Survivor', first published in *Perspectives* October 1994; Solar Navigator for the adapted text on p. 73 'Thor Heyerdahl and the Kon-Tiki Expedition' from http://www.solarnavigator.net/history/kontiki.htm. Reproduced by permission of Solar Navigator; John Robinson for the article on p. 85 'TV Music Programme' from 'Boogie Nights' *The Guardian* 13 October 2003. Reproduced by permission of John Robinson; Peter Fraser Dunlop for the article on p. 86 'Opera Audiences' from 'Quiet Please' by James Fenton, *The Guardian* 22 November 2003. Reprinted by permission of PFD on behalf of James Fenton. Copyright © Salamander Press, 2003; Independent News and Media Limited for the adapted article on p. 87 'U2 on tour in the USA' from 'My Crazy Life in U2' by Mark Ellen, *The Independent* 11 November 2005. Copyright © Independent News and Media Limited; Cosmopolitan Magazine for the article on p. 93 'Career Power' by Carole Pemberton. *Cosmopolitan Magazine*. Reproduced by permission of Cosmopolitan Magazine © National Magazine Company; AA Publishing for the text on p. 98 'Travelling through Norway' from *AA Great Railway Journeys of the World*. Reproduced by kind permission of the Automobile Association.

For permission to reproduce copyright photographs:

Arthur Robb for p. 10; Kevin Schafer/CORBIS for p. 37; NASA Images/Alamy for p. 89.

Colour section

Alamy/Kathy de Witt pC11 (tr), Alamy/Mark Glaister pC10 (tl), Alamy/Mediacolour pC11 (b), Alamy/OJO Images Ltd pC2 (tl), Alamy/Photofusion pC4 (b), Alamy/Woodystock pC5 (tl); **Art Directors & Trip**/M Jelliffe pC8 (bl); **Collections**/George Wright pC4 (tr), Collections/Roger Scruton pC1 (t); **Corbis**/George Shelly Inc pC2 (b), Corbis/Stephen Welstead pC11 (tl); **Getty Images** pC12 (tr), Getty Images/Hulton Archive pC12 (cl), Getty Images/Hulton Archives/Fox Photos pC12 (bl), Getty Images/Jeff Cadge pC4 (tl), Getty Images/Paul Chesley pC7 (b), Getty Images/Paul p C6 Souders (br); **John Birdsall** pC3 (all), pC8 (t); **Pictures Colour Library** pC6 (cr); **Punchstock**/Construction Photography pC10 (b), Punchstock/Corbis pC5 (b), Punchstock/Creatas Images pC6 (cl), Punchstock/Image Source pC5 (tr), Punchstock/Radius pC10 (tr), Punchstock/Stockbyte pC2 (tr); **Rex Features** pC1 (bl); **Robert Harding**/Jean Brooks pC6 (tl); **Royal Geographical Society**, London pC12 (cr); **Sally & Richard Greenhill**/Sally Greenhill pC1 (br), pC7 (tr), pC8 (br); **Science Photo Library**/Library of Congress pC12 (tl), Science Photo Library/NASA pC12 (br); **Tografox**/Bob Battersby pC7 (tl).

Picture research by Alison Prior

Design concept by Peter Ducker

Cover design by David Lawton

The recordings which accompany this book were made at Studio AVP, London

Introduction

This collection of four complete practice tests comprises papers from the University of Cambridge ESOL Examinations Certificate in Advanced English (CAE) examination; students can practise these tests on their own or with the help of a teacher.

The CAE examination is part of a suite of general English examinations produced by Cambridge ESOL. This suite consists of five examinations that have similar characteristics but are designed for different levels of English language ability. Within the five levels, CAE is at Level C1 in the Council of Europe's *Common European Framework of Reference for Languages: Learning, teaching, assessment*. It has also been accredited by the Qualifications and Curriculum Authority in the UK as a Level 2 ESOL certificate in the National Qualifications Framework. The CAE examination is widely recognised in commerce and industry and in individual university faculties and other educational institutions.

Examination	Council of Europe Framework Level	UK National Qualifications Framework Level
CPE Certificate of Proficiency in English	C2	3
CAE Certificate in Advanced English	C1	2
FCE First Certificate in English	B2	1
PET Preliminary English Test	B1	Entry 3
KET Key English Test	A2	Entry 2

Further information

The information contained in this practice book is designed to be an overview of the exam. For a full description of all of the above exams including information about task types, testing focus and preparation, please see the relevant handbooks which can be obtained from Cambridge ESOL at the address below or from the website at: www.CambridgeESOL.org

University of Cambridge ESOL Examinations
1 Hills Road
Cambridge CB1 2EU
United Kingdom

Telephone: +44 1223 553997
Fax: +44 1223 553621
e-mail: ESOLHelpdesk@ucles.org.uk

Introduction

The structure of CAE: an overview

The CAE examination consists of five papers.

Paper 1   Reading   1 hour 15 minutes
This paper consists of **four** parts, each containing one text or several shorter pieces. There are 34 questions in total, including multiple choice, gapped text and multiple matching.

Paper 2   Writing   1 hour 30 minutes
This paper consists of **two** parts which carry equal marks. In Part 1, which is **compulsory**, input material of up to 150 words is provided on which candidates have to base their answers. Candidates have to write either an article, a letter, a proposal, or a report of between 180 and 220 words.

In Part 2, there are four tasks from which candidates **choose one** to write about. The range of tasks from which questions may be drawn includes an article, a competition entry, a contribution to a longer piece, an essay, an information sheet, a letter, a proposal, a report and a review. The last question is based on the set books. These books remain on the list for two years. Look on the website, or contact the Cambridge ESOL Local Secretary in your area for the up-to-date list of set books. The question on the set books has two options from which candidates **choose one** to write about. In this part, candidates have to write between 220 and 260 words.

Paper 3   Use of English   1 hour
This paper consists of **five** parts and tests control of English grammar and vocabulary. There are 50 questions in total. The tasks include gap-filling exercises, word formation, lexical appropriacy and sentence transformation.

Paper 4   Listening   40 minutes (approximately)
This paper consists of **four** parts. Each part contains a recorded text or texts and some questions including multiple choice, sentence completion and multiple matching. There is a total of 30 questions. Each text is heard twice.

Paper 5   Speaking   15 minutes
This paper consists of **four** parts. The standard test format is two candidates and two examiners. One examiner takes part in the conversation while the other examiner listens. Both examiners give marks. Candidates will be given photographs and other visual and written material to look at and talk about. Sometimes candidates will talk with the other candidates, sometimes with the examiner and sometimes with both.

Grading

The overall CAE grade is based on the total score gained in all five papers. Each paper is weighted to 40 marks. Therefore, the five CAE papers total 200 marks, after weighting. It is not necessary to achieve a satisfactory level in all five papers in order to pass the examination. Certificates are given to candidates who pass the examination with grade A, B or C. A is the highest. D and E are failing grades. All candidates are sent a Statement of Results which includes a graphical profile of their performance in each paper and shows their relative performance in each one.

For further information on grading and results, go to the website (see page 5).

Test 1

PAPER 1 READING (1 hour 15 minutes)

Part 1

You are going to read three extracts which are all concerned in some way with human behaviour. For questions **1–6**, choose the answer (**A, B, C** or **D**) which you think fits best according to the text.

Mark your answers **on the separate answer sheet**.

Extract from a Book Review

Why do vast flocks of birds, driven as much by some irrepressible genetic impulse as by the dictates of seasonal change, migrate thousands of miles every year? And why do people, torn between 'the known and the new', so often oscillate between the prospect of the journey and the draw of home? Under the pretext of exploring the first question, *The Snow Geese*, William Fiennes's quirky and autobiographical first book, takes us to the heart of the second.

The story begins with Fiennes confined to a hospital bed, stricken by a curious and psychologically debilitating illness, dreaming of the comforts and protection of his family home. But when he returns to the familiarity of the old ironstone house, restlessness soon replaces homesickness. He longs to be jolted out of his introspection. Paul Gallico's novel *The Snow Goose* becomes an unlikely inspiration, and Fiennes resolves to follow the migratory path of real-life snow geese as they fly from Texas to the Canadian Arctic Circle on their annual spring voyage. It is emotional healing through the power of bird-watching, allowing him to put the past behind him. The result is an original blend of travel writing, autobiography and reportage.

1   In the first paragraph, the reviewer suggests that Fiennes' book

   A   seeks to understand people's mixed feelings about travel.
   B   throws new light on the migratory habits of birds.
   C   rejects comparisons between human and bird behaviour.
   D   fails to answer satisfactorily either of the questions it poses.

2   What do we learn about Fiennes in the second paragraph?

   A   His state of health prevents him from travelling.
   B   He has been inspired by a book he read in hospital.
   C   He is looking for something to occupy his mind positively.
   D   He has written his book as a way of overcoming his illness.

Tools

Anthropologists often say that what distinguishes humans from other primates is the ability to use tools. Unfortunately, they don't tell us how, while using those tools, the human in question – in this case yours truly – is supposed not to mislay them continually. As a qualified bricklayer, I should say at the outset that I never have a problem with my bricklaying tools. It was drummed into me that, when not in my hand, my trowel would be stuck in the pile of mortar on the spot board, my tape would be in my left-hand pocket, my spirit level would be leaning against the brick stack and my pencil behind my right ear. If I have even the slightest temptation to put these items anywhere else, then my instructor's voice jumps out from the recesses of my memory and gives me a loud ticking-off. So these tools are always to hand.

But, with other jobs, I've never been able to get into the same kind of habit. Screwdrivers, pincers, spanners – one minute I'm using them, the next they've disappeared. I can spend more time looking for a screwdriver than actually using it. Really tidy people hang their tools on hooks fixed to a pegboard on the wall of their workshop, and draw the outline of each tool with a felt-tipped pen, so they can see where everything belongs and spot if something is missing. I admire these people immensely, but something in my character prevents me ever doing this myself. I did once get as far as buying a sheet of pegboard, but then I mislaid it.

3   The writer attributes his tidiness with his bricklaying tools to

   A   his need to use them on a regular basis.
   B   the fact that he has a good memory.
   C   his years of experience in the trade.
   D   the effectiveness of his training.

4   In the piece as a whole, the writer is

   A   casting doubt on an academic theory.
   B   acknowledging his own shortcomings.
   C   making fun of people who are too tidy.
   D   explaining how tools should be maintained.

Book Crossing

My heart was thumping. Surreptitiously, I scanned the carriage. The train coasted into the platform, and the briefcase-clutching, umbrella-wielding crowd made its way towards the door. I slid my book – Hanif Kureishi's *Love in a Blue Time* – between two seats. A quick glance at my fellow passengers: no one saw. Off the train, and up the escalator – I increased my pace and pulled down my hat. Almost out of the station. I had done it! I had 'released' my first book. As my smile spread, I noticed rapidly approaching footsteps from behind. A tap on my shoulder: 'Excuse me, Miss,' said a kindly man, 'I think you left this behind.' Bother!

The Book Crossing organisation – nay, movement – claims, with 250,000 members globally, to be the largest book group in the world. Here's how it works. You register with the site (www.bookcrossing.com), tag one of your books with a special Book Crossing number generated by the website, and then 'release it to the wild'. With any luck, your book will then be rescued – or, as they say, captured. The book-catcher is invited, via use of the Book Crossing code number and website, to update the travels of the book, read and exchange their impressions of it and then, in true Book Crossing spirit, pass it on.

5   In the first paragraph, the writer describes a situation in which she

   A   felt short-lived satisfaction in an achievement.
   B   was embarrassed when her intentions were uncovered.
   C   became resigned to her inability to do something successfully.
   D   had feelings of frustration towards someone who intended to spoil her plans.

6   The organisation described in the second paragraph aims to

   A   promote the work of certain authors.
   B   encourage people to read online novels.
   C   provoke discussion of certain published works.
   D   persuade people to buy more books.

Test 1

Part 2

You are going to read an extract from a magazine article. Six paragraphs have been removed from the extract. Choose from the paragraphs **A–G** the one which fits each gap (**7–12**). There is one extra paragraph which you do not need to use.

Mark your answers **on the separate answer sheet**.

The Magic Lute

Four hundred years ago, the royal courts of Europe resounded to strains of the lute. Then the instrument did a mysterious vanishing act. Arthur Robb is one of a small band of craftsmen bringing the instrument back from the past.

Arthur Robb has been marching to a different tune all his life. When the youth of Europe was listening to the Beatles and the Rolling Stones, he went to Paris and Amsterdam as part of a classical choir. And then in swinging London, he discovered even earlier music. It has all been good training, though. Now in his fifties, he is recognised as a leading expert in one of contemporary music's most fashionable offshoots – the revival of interest in the ancient string instrument, the lute.

| 7 | |

Yet lutes were once produced in astonishing numbers. When the celebrated Italian lute maker Laux Mahler died in 1552, an inventory of his workshop revealed more than a thousand lutes in various stages of construction. The instrument's disappearance was so dramatic, however, that very few early examples survive.

| 8 | |

What happened to all the others is a mystery. Robb's theory is that the lute was killed off by the development of keyboard instruments like the pianoforte. But the end must have come suddenly. Some of the last music for solo lute was written by J.S. Bach. Within years of his death in 1750, the instrument which had dominated Europe's musical repertoire for centuries had all but vanished.

| 9 | |

Digging into literature and old manuscripts, such as early musical scores, has allowed him to discover how the music might have sounded, whilst the examination

of old paintings gives clues as to the details of the instrument's design. The lute has certainly altered over time, evolving from an elongated oval to a deep pear-shape. The stringing and the sound produced must also have changed as a result. 'The lute is like a time machine,' says Robb. 'Its history goes back into antiquity, possibly to ancient Egypt.'

| 10 | |

Lute music is considered rather quiet compared with the volume of today's orchestration. But centuries ago, when music was being written for the instrument, people's ears were better attuned to quieter sounds.

| 11 | |

Despite his enthusiasm, his initial efforts did not meet with immediate approval. A novice carpenter, he practised for a year, making wooden toys and household items to improve his basic skills, before joining an adult education class in musical instrument making. After months of meticulous work, he proudly offered a completed lute to a music shop in Bristol.

| 12 | |

Far from being discouraged, Robb set about putting things to rights. Modern-day lute makers have problems their craftsmen forebears could never have imagined. Worldwide concern about the use of rare timber, for example, has meant that he has had to adapt his methods to the materials that are most readily available. He has, however, gone on to make dozens of lutes, each finer than the last, and repaired many more.

A Those that do are now priceless museum pieces, and even these treasured relics have been damaged or altered so much during their life that copying them doesn't guarantee historical accuracy.

B What's more, no authentic plan of a genuine fifteenth- or sixteenth-century lute has ever been found, and so no one knows what tools were used to make the instruments. Robb, alongside fellow enthusiasts in Britain and the USA, has been spearheading the lute's revival. This means unearthing fragments of information from surrounding strata like archaeologists hunting a fossil.

C In turning it down, they left him in no doubt as to the shortcomings of his creation. It was the wrong shape, the wrong weight, the strings were too long to achieve the right pitch and the pegs which tightened the strings were too bulky for comfort.

D But so little factual evidence remains, even from more recent times, that Robb has to think himself back in time in order to begin to see how they should be made. Only by appreciating the way people lived, how they behaved and the technology they used, can he begin to piece together the complete picture.

E 'Appreciating small nuances like that is vital to an appreciation of how the instrument might have been played,' Robb says. As one of a small band of professional lute makers who keep in touch via the internet, Robb can share these impressions, as well as swapping problems and possible solutions. No such forum existed when Robb began to construct his first lute 25 years ago, however. He had to work things out on his own.

F Robb's enquiries have, however, punctured one other popular myth – that of the lute player as a wandering minstrel. Almost from its introduction into Europe, the lute was a wealthy person's instrument, the players attaining a status comparable to modern-day concert pianists.

G From a tiny attic workshop in the English countryside, Robb makes exquisite examples of this forgotten instrument. Piecing together the few remaining clues to the instrument's construction and musical characteristics has demanded all his single-minded concentration.

Part 3

You are going to read a magazine article. For questions **13–19**, choose the answer (**A, B, C** or **D**) which you think fits best according to the text.

Mark your answers **on the separate answer sheet**.

P.D. James

Barbara Michaels meets the acclaimed crime writer, whose innocent exterior hides a complex and brilliant imagination.

Best-selling crime writer P.D. James – the initials stand for Phyllis Dorothy – exudes an air of quiet authority. It is easy to envisage her, had she not become a creator of detective stories with more twists and turns than a spiral staircase, as a headmistress of a girls' school. But it is soon apparent from what she says that the authoritative mien is, in fact, a cloak for shyness. She reluctantly admits that Adam Dalgliesh, the detective in her novels, 'is, I suppose, modelled on myself – or rather, the way I would have turned out if I had been a man'. Dalgliesh prefers to unravel the complexities of crimes solo, as does his creator. 'I need time on my own, particularly when I am writing. I can write more or less anywhere as long as I have total privacy.'

She is too modest to concur with the view that she is Britain's best-known crime writer, even though her books – 12 major detective novels – are read avidly by millions all over the world. She herself is a great fan of the works of close friend Ruth Rendell. 'I particularly enjoy her psychological works, written under the name of Barbara Vine.' Books beside her bed are most likely to be by women writers such as Iris Murdoch, Anita Brookner and Penelope Lively, although not to the total exclusion of male authors like Graham Greene and Evelyn Waugh, whom she considers to have been the greatest novelists of their generation.

Success came to P.D. James late in life. Now in her seventies, she was 42 when her first crime novel, *Cover Her Face*, was published. Born in Oxford, the eldest of three children, Phyllis grew up mainly in Cambridge, where her family moved when she was 11 years old. 'I met my husband there – he was a student at the university, and I have always loved the place. That is why I chose it as the setting for *An Unsuitable Job For A Woman*.'

Reluctantly, she reveals that from a promising start, life has been hard, even tragic at times. Her Irish doctor husband, Connor Bantry White, returned from the Second World War, during which he served with the Royal Army Medical Corps, a very sick man. 'I had to work long hours to support him and our two young daughters, Clare and Jane. The ideas were teeming in my head, but I could do practically nothing about it – I simply hadn't the time. My husband's parents, however, were marvellous, and took my daughters under their wing, giving them a sense of security throughout those difficult years.'

While working full-time in administration for the National Health Service, she made good use of her enviable organisational skills. At one point, five psychiatric outpatients' clinics came under her jurisdiction. Then followed 11 years at the Home Office, first in the Police Department, doing administration for forensic science research, and then in the Criminal Law section, in the juvenile crime division. It was while working in forensic science that she became 'quite accustomed' to the sight of corpses. But it was not fascination with death itself that inspired her. 'It was, rather, the shape and construction involved in the writing of a crime novel that appealed. I have always enjoyed reading detective stories, and I always knew that I wanted to be a writer.'

'I didn't want to use the traumatic events of my own life in a work of fiction. The writing of a detective story appealed as a wonderful apprenticeship for someone setting out to be a serious novelist, and it was suitably removed from my own experience. As I went on, I became increasingly aware that one could stay within the constraints and indeed within the so-called formula of the classic detective story and still write a good, serious and revealing novel about human beings. 'Writing detective stories', she says, 'is a way of bringing order out of disorder. The solution of a crime confirms the sanctity of life – even if that life is unlovable. Nobody really likes violence.'

13 What does the writer suggest about P.D. James's outward manner?

   A It is an attempt to discourage curiosity.
   B It points to a lack of self-confidence.
   C It conceals the true nature of her personality.
   D It comes as a surprise to her readers.

14 When questioned about Adam Dalgliesh, P.D. James

   A concedes that the detective resembles her.
   B admits that his behaviour is unusual.
   C accepts that he does not enjoy company.
   D recognises a weakness in the detective's character.

15 What is revealed about P.D. James's tastes in reading?

   A She prefers books with lots of action.
   B She is less keen on male than female writers.
   C She believes that men write better books than women.
   D She thinks that women writers are not given enough credit.

16 According to P.D. James, her early writing career suffered from lack of

   A support.
   B commitment.
   C confidence.
   D opportunity.

17 What characterised P.D. James's work in the National Health Service?

   A It was well-suited to her talents.
   B It was not a satisfying experience.
   C It was useful for her future writing.
   D It was not sufficiently demanding.

18 P.D. James was drawn to writing crime novels because

   A they were her favourite sort of reading.
   B they would be useful to her in her career.
   C she liked the technical challenge they offered.
   D she had experienced the effects of crime at first hand.

19 What realisation did P.D. James come to while working on her detective stories?

   A It was not necessary to pay attention to established patterns.
   B The conventions did not adversely affect the quality of her writing.
   C It was inevitable that she would become emotionally involved.
   D The subject matter was more limiting than she had expected.

Test 1

Part 4

You are going to read an introduction to a book about how to organise local events. For questions **20–34**, choose from the sections of the introduction (**A–E**). The sections may be chosen more than once.

Mark your answers **on the separate answer sheet**.

In which section(s) of the text are the following mentioned?

the importance of making it clear to people that you value them	20 ___
the writer's natural instinct to want to do everything herself	21 ___
times when the writer has felt she may become unable to cope	22 ___
a way in which the writer's situation has been different from that of people she has worked with	23 ___
people who get involved in organising events but don't really want to do any work	24 ___
some people preferring others to be in charge	25 ___
the assistance provided by people who are physically strong	26 ___
people who get involved because of their strongly-held views	27 ___ 28 ___
a situation in which you are free to concentrate only on the most important aspects of organising an event	29 ___
the willingness of people to try things they may not have done before	30 ___
the feeling that you really are in control, not just pretending to be	31 ___
the writer's belief that she cannot tell readers everything they need to know	32 ___
the difference that may exist between the way events are planned and the way they turn out	33 ___
a situation when it is desirable to have someone else checking what you are doing	34 ___

Organising local events

Are you thinking of setting up a fundraising event for your local school or community? Sarah Passingham, a professional fundraiser, offers advice.

A

I have had a lot of fun from running events; it has been hard work but I have always done it in the knowledge that I was being paid for my many hours of toil. There are hundreds, probably thousands, of volunteers who work just as hard for no financial remuneration at all, and I have enormous admiration for them. I have worked with a good many groups and individuals who have had a burning ambition to do something for a particular community, remaining enthusiastic even in the face of adversity. When things go wrong, it is desperately disappointing and disheartening. Perhaps by looking at some of my suggestions and learning from my mistakes, most of those disappointing times can be averted. However, this guide is not meant as the definitive work on organising events; rather it is meant as a framework on which to hang your own ideas and methods of doing things.

B

A very important piece of advice is: Don't panic! Organising events can be a fraught business and I have myself come close to falling apart on occasions, but it achieved nothing and did not inspire my colleagues. I hope this book will act as a buffer – to be used before you go off the rails! – and that it will allow you not only to appear calm and well organised, but genuinely to be those things. In nearly 10 years of working with every type of professional and amateur, indoors and out, when plans have moved from A to B and sometimes to C due to bad weather or other reasons too numerous to mention, I don't think the general public have ever realised what was going on behind the scenes. Sometimes what they were experiencing was far removed from the original concept but nobody minded and, more often than not, nobody knew.

C

Even if you have unlimited spare time and resources to set an event up, it is almost impossible to organise the day itself with only one person. You physically cannot be in two or more places at once. Committees can be tiresome, unwieldy groups of people who may have come out for the evening just to enjoy some social chit-chat. However, if you have a committee that operates efficiently and decisively, it can relieve you of much of the time-consuming but necessary work, and allow you to get to grips with the real nitty-gritty and keep a good overview without getting bogged down by details. And when you are dealing with money from the public, it is always worth having at least a cashier or treasurer as a second person to keep an eye on your balance or banking. You never want to be put in the position of having the finger of doubt or suspicion pointed at you, even if you know that you are entirely innocent.

D

When I first started, my critics would say that one of my failings was an unwillingness to delegate. I hope that is no longer true, as in time I have come to realise the value of help, especially from the volunteer. Help can come in many forms apart from the obvious muscle and brawn. Support, encouragement and an infectious enthusiasm all come from working with people who have chosen to give their time and sometimes their belongings for a cause they care passionately about. But what can you expect from volunteers? There is one rule of thumb here. Let volunteers know exactly what job it is that they are volunteering for. They can then make the choice to put themselves forward or not. But don't expect anyone to do anything you would not be prepared to tackle yourself!

E

In my experience, as long as they are prepared beforehand, people will have a go at almost anything. Of course, you have to be able to rely on your volunteers once they have offered their services. You need commitment from them, and if they can't make it on a particular day or are going to be late, you need to know well in advance so that you can make alternative arrangements. Now, what's in it for them? Fun, companionship, a sense of responsibility or, conversely, allowing someone else to hold responsibility, or simply an opportunity to get out of the house. But, above all, we all need to feel needed and you will often find that the more you show that you need your volunteers, the more they will be prepared to commit their time and energy to you, often time and time again. If you, as leader, keep the atmosphere as light as possible by sharing the decisions and being flexible, they will manage to get what they want out of the work and you will get a job well done.

Test 1

PAPER 2 WRITING (1 hour 30 minutes)

Part 1

You **must** answer this question. Write your answer in **180–220** words in an appropriate style.

---

1   You are the secretary of the Sports Club at an international college in New Zealand. The club would like to make some improvements and needs financial help from the college. The college Principal, Dr Parker, has asked you to write a report on the club. Some of the students have given you their views.

Read the advertisement for the club and comments from the students below. Then, **using the information appropriately**, write a report for the Principal, suggesting what changes you would like to make and why and persuading him to contribute some money towards these changes.

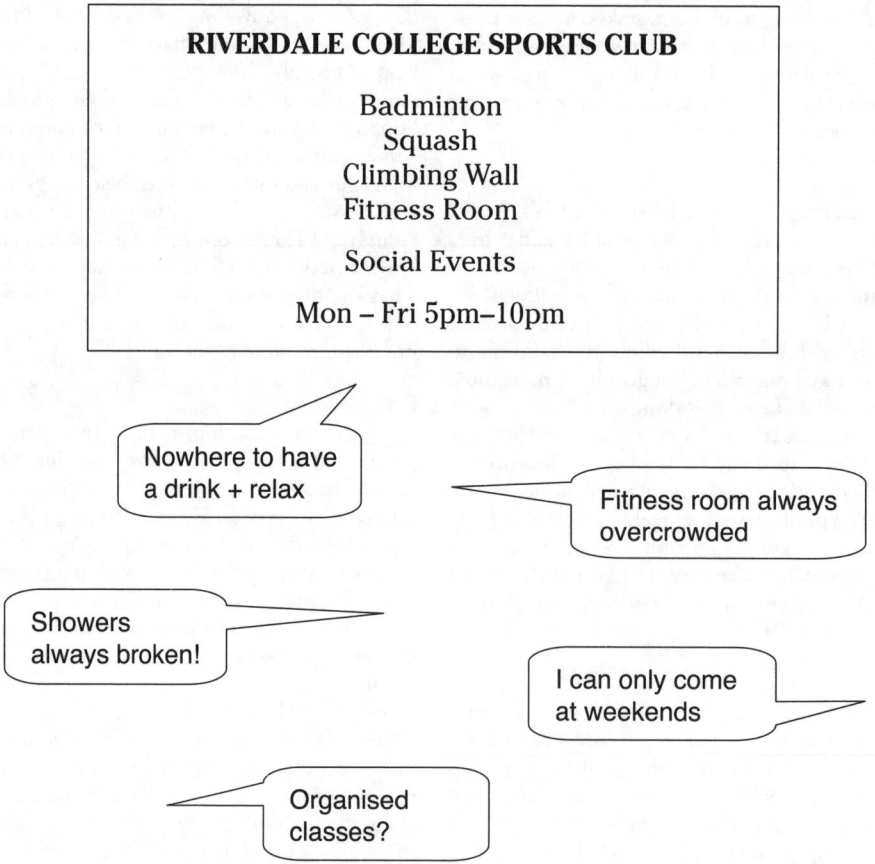

Now write your **report** for the Principal, as outlined above. You should use your own words as far as possible.

Part 2

Choose **one** of the following writing tasks. Your answer should follow exactly the instructions given. Write approximately **220–260** words.

2   You see the announcement below in *Modern World*, an international magazine.

> ### NEW TECHNOLOGY AND YOU
>
> We invite you, our readers, to submit an article on new technology and how it affects your life. We will publish one article from each country. Your article should outline the impact of new technology on your life now. You should also explain what further changes are likely to take place in the near future and how these could affect you.

Write your **article**.

3   You see this competition in an English language magazine.

> If you really want to learn English you should get a job in an English-speaking country, speak to the people and travel around.
> Do you agree with this opinion? Give us your reasons why or why not. The best answer will win a ticket to London.

Write your **competition entry**, giving your views.

4   You have been discussing sports sponsorship in class, and your teacher has asked you to write an essay on the following subject.

> *Many sports teams and sporting events depend on sponsorship from the world of business. Does this link between sport and business have a positive or negative effect on sport?*

Write your **essay**.

5   Answer **one** of the following two questions based on **one** of the titles below.

(a) Adriana Trigiani: *Big Stone Gap*

Your local college library wants to extend its collection of humorous novels. The librarian has heard *Big Stone Gap* described as 'hilarious'. She has asked you to write a report on *Big Stone Gap*, describing the two scenes which you found most amusing and explaining why.

Write your **report**.

(b) Dick Francis: *In the Frame*

You have been asked to write a review of *In the Frame* for your college magazine. In your review you should describe Charles Todd and comment on whether you think the story would appeal to students at your college, giving reasons for your opinions.

Write your **review**.

Test 1

PAPER 3 USE OF ENGLISH (1 hour)

Part 1

For questions **1–12**, read the text below and decide which answer (**A, B, C** or **D**) best fits each gap. There is an example at the beginning (**0**).

Mark your answers **on the separate answer sheet**.

Example:

0 A deals   **B** handles   **C** runs   **D** controls

| 0 | A | **B** | C | D |

Secretaries

What's in a name? In the case of the secretary, or Personal Assistant (PA), it can be something rather surprising. The dictionary calls a secretary 'anyone who **(0)** ..... correspondence, keeps records and does clerical work for others'. But while this particular job **(1)** ..... looks a bit **(2)** ....., the word's original meaning is a hundred times more exotic and perhaps more **(3)** .... The word itself has been with us since the 14th century and comes from the mediaeval Latin word *secretarius* meaning 'something hidden'. Secretaries started out as those members of staff with knowledge hidden from others, the silent ones mysteriously **(4)** ..... the secret machinery of organisations.

Some years ago 'something hidden' probably meant **(5)** ..... out of sight, tucked away with all the other secretaries and typists. A good secretary was an unremarkable one, efficiently **(6)** ..... orders, and then returning mouse-like to his or her station behind the typewriter, but, with the **(7)** ..... of new office technology, the job **(8)** ..... upgraded itself and the role has changed to one closer to the original meaning. The skills required are more demanding and more technical. Companies are **(9)** ..... that secretarial staff should already be **(10)** ..... trained in, and accustomed to working with, a **(11)** ..... of word processing packages. Professionals in the **(12)** ..... business point out that nowadays secretarial staff may even need some management skills to take on administration, personnel work and research.

18

1	A	explanation	B	detail	C	definition	D	characteristic
2	A	elderly	B	unfashionable	C	outdated	D	aged
3	A	characteristic	B	related	C	likely	D	appropriate
4	A	operating	B	pushing	C	functioning	D	effecting
5	A	kept	B	covered	C	packed	D	held
6	A	satisfying	B	obeying	C	completing	D	minding
7	A	advent	B	approach	C	entrance	D	opening
8	A	truly	B	validly	C	correctly	D	effectively
9	A	insisting	B	ordering	C	claiming	D	pressing
10	A	considerably	B	highly	C	vastly	D	supremely
11	A	group	B	collection	C	cluster	D	range
12	A	appointment	B	hiring	C	recruitment	D	engagement

Part 2

For questions **13–27**, read the text below and think of the word which best fits each gap. Use only **one** word in each gap. There is an example at the beginning (**0**).

Write your answers **IN CAPITAL LETTERS on the separate answer sheet**.

Example: `0` `T` `H` `E`

Changing cities

What will the city of (**0**) ..... future look like? This question has been asked (**13**) ..... many times in recent history – and answered inconclusively (**14**) ..... equal number of times – that we (**15**) ..... be sure of (**16**) ..... thing only: no one can predict with (**17**) ..... degree of accuracy how cities will look 50 or 500 years from now.

The reason is simple – cities are (**18**) ..... a continual state of change. Over the (**19**) ..... fifty years they have changed so rapidly that the oldest residents will remember a time (**20**) ..... their city seemed to belong not just to another era (**21**) ..... to a different dimension.

(**22**) ..... is true both of planned and unplanned cities. Planned cities such as New York and Paris, (**23**) ..... are closely organised on a grid or diagram of streets and avenues, have effectively burst at the seams this century, while unplanned cities such as Tokyo and Los Angeles have grown just (**24**) ..... dramatically. Although their centres might remain much as they were many years (**25**) ..... , their suburbs have spread (**26**) ..... the tentacles of an octopus.

Some economists argue that expansion is a sign of a healthy economy (**27**) ..... that it is expanding cities that attract international investment.

Part 3

For questions **28–37**, read the text below. Use the word given in capitals at the end of some of the lines to form a word that fits in the gap **in the same line**. There is an example at the beginning (**0**).

Write your answers **IN CAPITAL LETTERS** on the separate answer sheet.

Example: | 0 | S | T | R | A | I | G | H | T | F | O | R | W | A | R | D | | | |

Snow-kiting: an alternative form of skiing?

Skiing is one of the most **(0)** ..... forms of exercise there is. It offers	**STRAIGHT**
the participant, whether a novice or an old hand at the sport, a great	
deal of excitement and **(28)** ..... , plus lots of fresh air. But skiing does	**PLEASE**
have its various **(29)** ..... . When it comes to guaranteeing a	**ADVANTAGE**
profitable day's downhill skiing, there are two essential ingredients.	
You need hills, or **(30)** ..... mountains, in order to get the most out	**PREFER**
of this **(31)** ..... ; then you need a fairly generous covering of snow.	**PURSUE**
(32) ..... , there are usually snow machines to supplement	**FORTUNE**
any natural **(33)** ..... in the supply of this second	**DEFICIENT**
(34) ..... , and help may now be at hand too for those lacking in	**REQUIRE**
the first, through the sport of snow-kiting.	

Snow-kiting is a wintry offshoot of kite-surfing, an established watersport. By harnessing their skis to an inflated kite, snow-kiters can move at speed across even the very flattest of landscapes. All

they need is a **(35)** ..... wind, then they can enjoy all the	**REASON**
exhilaration of a fast downhill ski run. In fact, partly because of	
(36) ..... objects such as electricity pylons and trees, the best	**HAZARD**
location for snow-kiting is not a ski resort at all – but a vast	
(37) ..... plain. Skiing may never be the same again.	**INTERRUPT**

Test 1

Part 4

For questions **38–42**, think of **one** word only which can be used appropriately in all three sentences. Here is an example (**0**).

Example:

0 The committee decided to .... the money equally between the two charities.

I can't believe that John and Maggie have decided to .... up after 20 years of marriage.

To serve a watermelon you need to .... it down the centre with a sharp knife.

Example: | 0 | S | P | L | I | T | | | | | | | | | | |

Write **only** the missing word **IN CAPITAL LETTERS on the separate answer sheet**.

---

38 Throughout the match, Philip .... the ball much harder than his opponent did.

Consumers were badly .... by price increases during the last economic crisis.

It suddenly .... him that today was a public holiday and all the shops would be shut.

39 The lake is rather .... this winter – we need more rain.

The critics seem to have a pretty .... opinion of his acting skills.

The manager's personal assistant came in to the meeting and spoke to him in a .... voice.

40 In the future we will be obtaining an increasing amount of .... from wind and water.

He did everything in his .... to find us somewhere to live.

Leaders are often unwilling to give up .... , even when they are very old.

41 The book about wildlife in the Antarctic .... me very deeply and I've been involved in conservation issues ever since I read it.

The politician's speech .... on several topics, but he mainly talked about inner city development.

When Sally .... the painting in the art gallery, all the alarms went off.

42 I wanted to study IT but there wasn't a .... on any of the courses.

The young Kenyan runner stumbled during the race and had to make do with second ....

I wish Nina would tidy up; she leaves her clothes all over the ....

Part 5

For questions **43–50**, complete the second sentence so that it has a similar meaning to the first sentence, using the word given. **Do not change the word given**. You must use between **three** and **six** words, including the word given. Here is an example (**0**).

Example:

0 Fernanda refused to wear her sister's old dress.

   NOT

   Fernanda said that .... her sister's old dress.

The gap can be filled with the words 'she would not wear', so you write:

Example: | **0** | SHE WOULD NOT WEAR

Write the missing words **IN CAPITAL LETTERS** on the separate answer sheet.

---

43 He's likely to lose his job if he keeps disagreeing with his boss.

   DANGER

   If he keeps disagreeing with his boss, he's .... from his job.

44 Although the children weren't listening, the teacher didn't get angry.

   ATTENTION

   Although the children weren't .... saying, the teacher didn't get angry.

45 Given that he has no experience, will Glyn be able to do this job?

   AFFECT

   Will Glyn's .... ability to do this job?

46 'Remember to write or phone,' Marta said as she waved goodbye to her friend.

TOUCH

'Don't ………………………………………………… ,' Marta said as she waved goodbye to her friend.

47 No changes will be made to this project.

AHEAD

This project will ………………………………………………… to plan.

48 He no longer thinks he can find a job before the end of the year.

HOPE

He has given ………………………………………………… a job before the end of the year.

49 It's difficult to know what my reaction would have been in that situation.

HOW

I'm not ………………………………………………… in that situation.

50 I don't expect the company to make a profit this year, given the economic climate.

SURPRISED

Given the economic climate, ………………………………………………… the company make a profit this year.

Test 1

PAPER 4 LISTENING (approximately 40 minutes)

Part 1

You will hear three different extracts. For questions **1–6**, choose the answer (**A**, **B** or **C**) which fits best according to what you hear. There are two questions for each extract.

Extract One

You overhear two friends, Gordon and Annabelle, discussing a film called *A Secret Place*, which they have both seen recently.

1 What do Gordon and Annabelle agree about?

   A The film lacks a coherent storyline.

   B The director was over-ambitious in his aims.

   C The book which the film was based on is far subtler.

2 What does Annabelle think about the film's ending?

   A It is greatly enhanced by the musical soundtrack.

   B It strikes a good balance between humour and tragedy.

   C It is a clever way of solving a character's problem.

Extract Two

You hear part of a radio interview with an architect called Alan Fasman.

3 Alan refers to St Paul's Cathedral in London because

   A it is a building of outstanding beauty.

   B it retains a powerful symbolism.

   C it met with disapproval at first.

4 How does Alan account for the success of public architecture in the Netherlands?

   A People there are very well informed about architecture.

   B Decision-making about architecture is well organised there.

   C Many of the world's leading architects happen to come from there.

Paper 4 Listening

Extract Three

You hear part of a radio interview with the ecologist Lorna Hindle about climate change.

5   What prompted Lorna to begin her latest project?

   A   dismay over a colleague's behaviour

   B   frustration at government inactivity

   C   concern about industrial pollution

6   What is Lorna's attitude to climate change?

   A   She believes individuals can help to combat it.

   B   She considers its dangers have been exaggerated.

   C   She places most emphasis on its economic implications.

Test 1

Part 2

You will hear a mountaineer called Stella Prime talking about her experience of climbing Mount Everest in the Himalayas. For questions **7–14**, complete the sentences.

Stella Prime: mountaineer

On her first expedition, Stella became aware of feelings of

| *and* | **7** | connected with mountaineering.

Stella had previously taken part in several so-called | | **8**

Stella found the | | **9** | for climbing Everest particularly hard.

On her second expedition, Stella was worried about the

| | **10** | she would have to climb through.

Stella had regretted taking

| | **11** | with her on her first expedition.

Stella says that she didn't take a

| | **12** | with her beyond a certain altitude.

Stella uses the word | | **13** | to describe the feelings of her party on reaching the summit.

Stella's book about her experiences is entitled | | **14**

Part 3

You will hear part of an interview with a man called Tony Elliott who founded a magazine called *Time Out*. For questions **15–20**, choose the answer (**A**, **B**, **C** or **D**) which fits best according to what you hear.

15 Tony says that *Time Out* was unlike other publications in 1968 because

   A   it was written by one person.
   B   information was more accurate.
   C   it had a comprehensive list of events.
   D   it was in the form of a magazine.

16 What experience did Tony have of publishing?

   A   He had worked for *What's On*.
   B   He had written numerous articles.
   C   He had transformed an existing magazine.
   D   He had started a student magazine.

17 Why did Tony leave university?

   A   He wanted to go to France.
   B   He didn't have time to study.
   C   He had failed his French examinations.
   D   He had found an alternative career.

18 According to Tony, what led to the magazine becoming a weekly?

   A   some market research
   B   the quantity of information
   C   technical improvements
   D   external pressure

19 Tony says the big publishers were not interested in this type of magazine because

   A   it was popular with students.
   B   it was considered too expensive.
   C   it came out too frequently.
   D   it threatened their publications.

20 Tony says that, compared to 1968, people who buy *Time Out* today are

   A   more intelligent and active.
   B   more likely to be parents.
   C   more or less the same age.
   D   more mature and professional.

Part 4

You will hear five short extracts in which people are talking about things that have recently happened to them at work.

TASK ONE

For questions **21–25**, choose from the list **A–H** what each speaker is talking about.

A receiving an unwelcome visitor

B being unfairly blamed for something

C making a terrible mistake

D receiving an unexpected offer

E doing something uncharacteristic

F resolving a misunderstanding

G avoiding an argument

H changing an opinion of someone

Speaker 1 [21]
Speaker 2 [22]
Speaker 3 [23]
Speaker 4 [24]
Speaker 5 [25]

While you listen you must complete both tasks.

TASK TWO

For questions **26–30**, choose from the list **A–H** the feeling each speaker is expressing.

A amusement

B anger

C guilt

D confusion

E resignation

F shock

G suspicion

H sadness

Speaker 1 [26]
Speaker 2 [27]
Speaker 3 [28]
Speaker 4 [29]
Speaker 5 [30]

PAPER 5 SPEAKING (15 minutes)

There are two examiners. One (the interlocutor) conducts the test, providing you with the necessary materials and explaining what you have to do. The other examiner (the assessor) is introduced to you, but then takes no further part in the interaction.

Part 1 (3 minutes)

The interlocutor first asks you and your partner a few questions. The interlocutor asks candidates for some information about themselves, then widens the scope of the questions by asking about, e.g. candidates' leisure activities, studies, travel and daily life. Candidates are expected to respond to the interlocutor's questions, and listen to what their partner has to say.

Part 2 (a one-minute 'long turn' for each candidate, plus 30-second response from the second candidate)

You are each given the opportunity to talk for about a minute, and to comment briefly after your partner has spoken.

The interlocutor gives you a set of pictures and asks you to talk about them for about one minute. It is important to listen carefully to the interlocutor's instructions. The interlocutor then asks your partner a question about your pictures and your partner responds briefly.

You are then given another set of pictures to look at. Your partner talks about these pictures for about one minute. This time the interlocutor asks you a question about your partner's pictures and you respond briefly.

Part 3 (approximately 4 minutes)

In this part of the test you and your partner are asked to talk together. The interlocutor places a new set of pictures on the table between you. This stimulus provides the basis for a discussion. The interlocutor explains what you have to do.

Part 4 (approximately 4 minutes)

The interlocutor asks some further questions, which leads to a more general discussion of what you have talked about in Part 3. You may comment on your partner's answers if you wish.

Visual materials for the Speaking test

What responsibilities do the members of the groups have?
How might they depend on each other?

Visual materials for the Speaking test

**What significance might the pieces of paper have?
How might the people be feeling?**

Visual materials for the Speaking test

**How might our attitudes towards these things change at different stages of our lives?
What might be the greatest priority at each of these stages?**

Visual materials for the Speaking test

How important is it for these people to be accurate? What might happen if they were not?

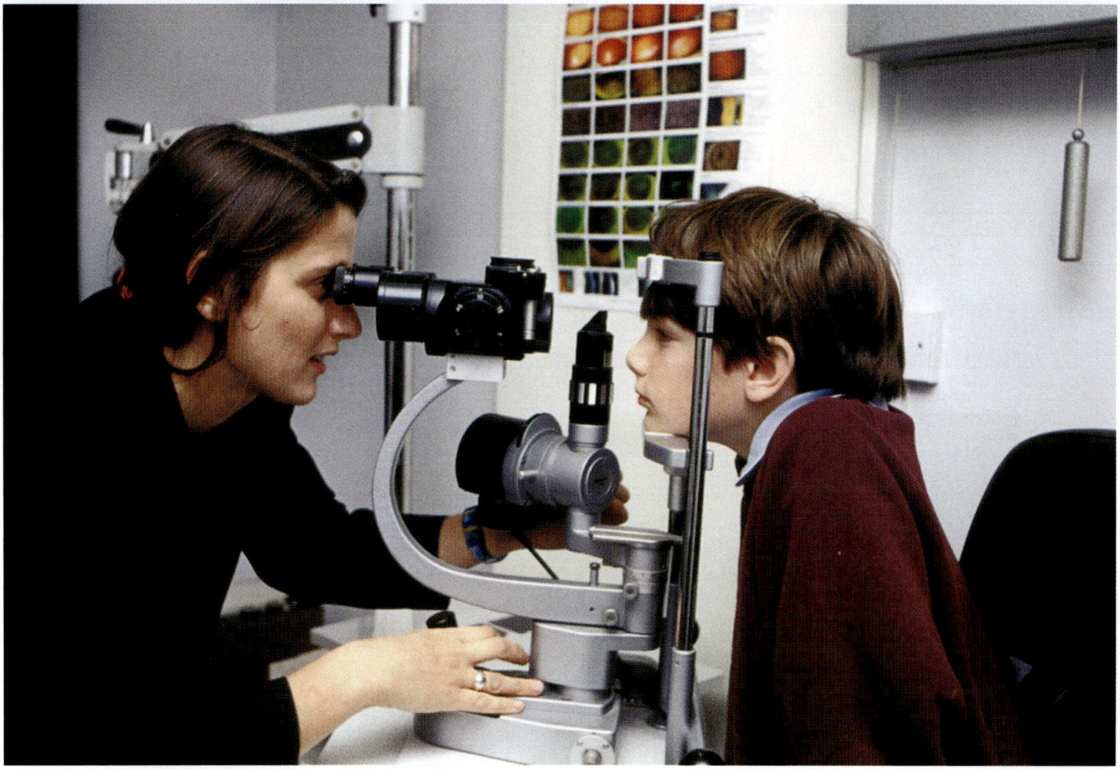

Visual materials for the Speaking test

Why might these possessions be important to these people?
How might the people feel if they no longer had them?

C5

Visual materials for the Speaking test

How successful might these designs be in raising awareness of the environment?
Which design would be most appropriate for the T-shirt?

Visual materials for the Speaking test

**What significance might the flowers have for these people?
How might they be feeling?**

Visual materials for the Speaking test

What might these people be observing?
Why might they be observing these things?

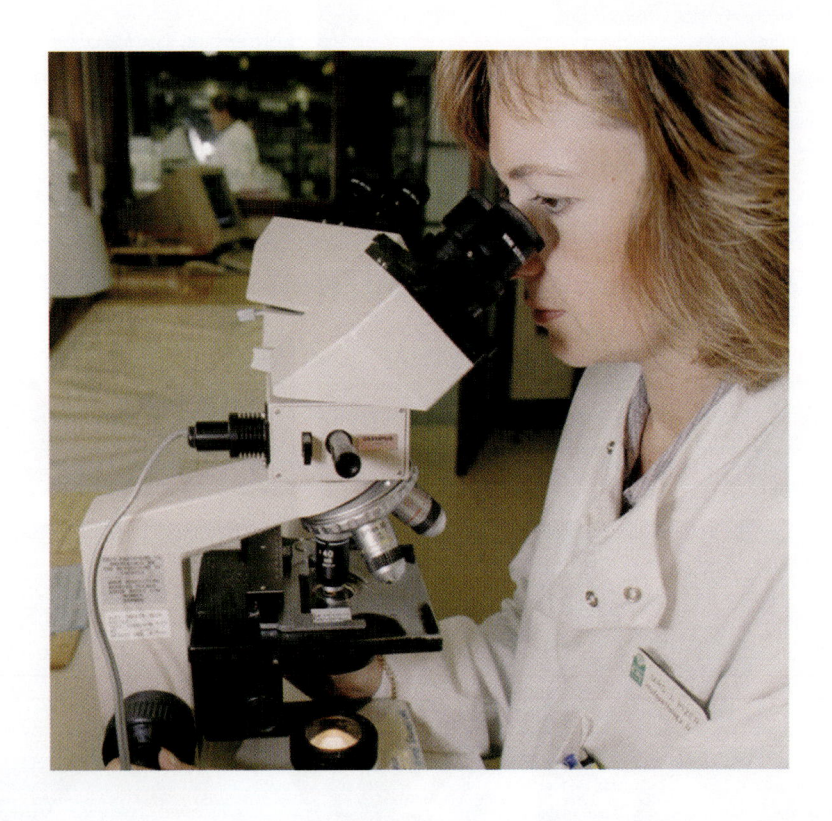

C8

Visual materials for the Speaking test

How effective might these ideas be in encouraging understanding between cultures?
Which two would be the most effective?

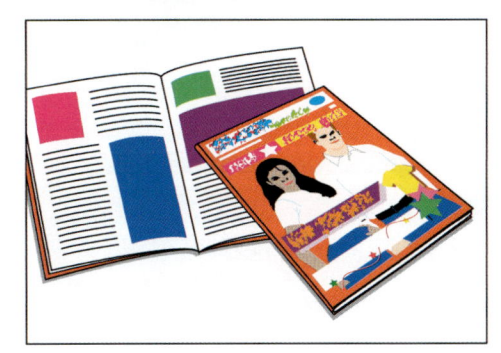

Visual materials for the Speaking test

How might the people be feeling?
How difficult might it have been to take the photograph?

Visual materials for the Speaking test

Why might these people have fallen asleep?
How might they feel when they wake up?

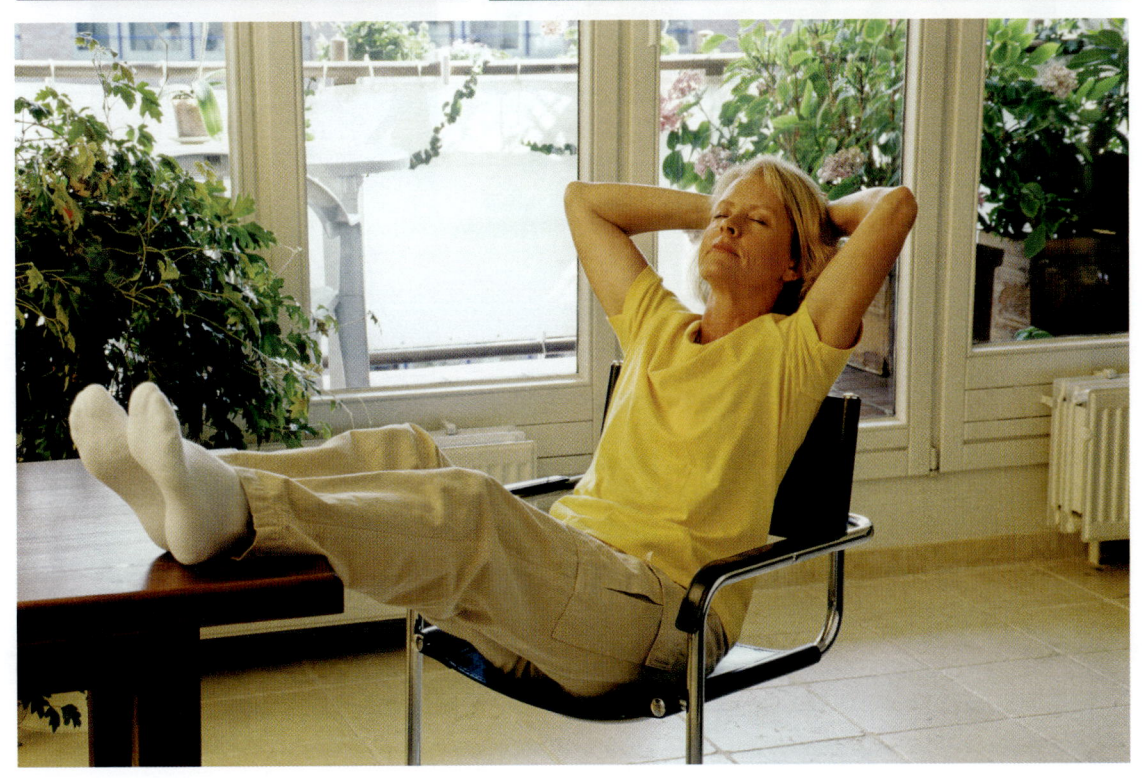

C11

Visual materials for the Speaking test

What effect have each of these events had on the world?
Which one has had the greatest influence on people's lives?

Test 2

PAPER 1 READING (1 hour 15 minutes)

Part 1

You are going to read three extracts which are all concerned in some way with well-being. For questions **1–6**, choose the answer (**A**, **B**, **C** or **D**) which you think fits best according to the text.

Mark your answers **on the separate answer sheet**.

A Martial Art

Learning expertise in Japanese martial arts has its price – bruised legs are standard badges of honour. But with perseverance these disciplines can boost mental alertness and physical strength, and relieve tension. As a novice I found there was a bewildering variety of martial arts. There were plenty that adopted seemingly aggressive methods of subduing an opponent, but they didn't appeal to me. I preferred something less belligerent, and I eventually discovered there was another way – that of aikido.

Aikido's founder was Morihei Ueshiba, a man who drew on ancient martial art styles and perfected his art in Japan in the 20th century. It's claimed he once pinned a famous sumo wrestler to the ground using just one finger. While that may be something of a fable, it illustrates aikido's core philosophy – overcoming opponents without doing them dire physical harm. Aikido is also effective training for strength, flexibility and posture. To be allowed on the exercise mats, you'll need the proper pyjama-like training wear and, as Paul Weber, a teacher of aikido, advises, 'an open mind. Leave all your preconceptions at the door.' Today, dozens of schools continue Ueshiba's teachings, so why not try it for yourself?

1 What was the writer's main complaint about martial arts?

    A the difficulty of finding one that attracted him
    B the physical pain caused by the exercises
    C the problem he had in restraining aggressive opponents
    D the time it took to learn the disciplines

2 According to the article, newcomers to aikido are recommended to

    A buy their equipment from a recognised source.
    B learn about the philosophy of Morihei Ueshiba.
    C go to classes without any fixed ideas about aikido.
    D check on their general health before attending classes.

Ecotourism

Snacking on green ants is not everyone's idea of the most delicious holiday indulgence, but on a recent walk through the Daintree rainforest in Queensland, Australia, Aboriginal guide Kirsty Norris assured a group of uncertain guests that the traditional food source of her Kuku Yalanji tribe was worth a try. She might have been right – but luckily for the native ants and the tourists, rain came streaming down through the canopy, sending any possible food scurrying for cover.

Connecting with nature isn't a compulsory part of a stay at an environmentally friendly resort, but at the Daintree Eco Lodge, where tree-house villas are set on stilts above the compound's waterfall-fed creek, many people find themselves doing a bit of communing while they relax.

Although ecotourism is increasing in popularity, recording heady growth worldwide, it is still difficult to define. For some travellers, ecotourism means eavesdropping on nature from the comfort of a plush bed with a magnificent view. For others, it's about doing without hot showers and trekking across wildernesses. However, industry watchers say the category's basic tenet is minimal environmental impact combined with some contribution to education and conservation.

3   What does the writer say about a stay at Daintree Eco Lodge?

    A   Visitors can choose how close to nature they get.
    B   The visitors' rooms are less luxurious than at other resorts.
    C   Visitors to the resort find the weather quite unpredictable.
    D   Most visitors enjoy the educational aspect of staying in the resort.

4   What point is made in the third paragraph?

    A   Ecotourism will soon reach a peak of popularity.
    B   Some areas of the world should be protected from ecotourists.
    C   The facilities provided for clients need to be improved.
    D   Ecotourism now follows some fundamental principles.

The happiest country

The most deservedly happy place on the planet is the South Pacific island nation of Vanuatu, according to an index published recently. Vanuatu comes top because its people are happy with their lot, live to nearly 70 and do little damage to the planet. Said Marke Lowen of Vanuatu Online, the country's online newspaper, 'People are generally happy here because they get by on very little. This is not a consumer-driven society. Life here is about community and family and goodwill to other people. It's a place where you don't worry too much.'

The Economics Foundation, who compiled the index, said that the small population of 200,000 and the lack of aggressive marketing in what is essentially a subsistence economy were other factors which elevated the country to its top-dog status, adding that people in Vanuatu considered themselves 'caretakers' of the land. The Foundation believes that the survey shows that people can live long, fulfilled lives without using more than their fair share of the Earth's resources.

5   What does Marke Lowen say about the people of Vanuatu?

   A   They are contented because everyone has a good income.
   B   They are happy because they live in a small community.
   C   They are glad to be isolated from the rest of the world.
   D   They are satisfied that they have everything they need.

6   The Economics Foundation has succeeded in

   A   demonstrating a point regarding national lifestyles.
   B   explaining their theory about the impact of marketing.
   C   finding new ways of minimising environmental damage.
   D   measuring the effectiveness of the economy in several countries.

Part 2

You are going to read an extract from a magazine article. Six paragraphs have been removed from the extract. Choose from the paragraphs **A–G** the one which fits each gap (**7–12**). There is one extra paragraph which you do not need to use.

Mark your answers **on the separate answer sheet**.

Chewing gum culture

It's fashionable, classless and Americans chew 12 million sticks of it a day. Discover how an ancient custom became big business.

Chewing gum contains fewer than ten calories per stick, but it is classified as a food and must therefore conform to the standards of the American Food and Drug Administration.

Today's gum is largely synthetic, with added pine resins and softeners which help to hold the flavour and improve the texture.

| 7 |

American colonists followed the example of the Amero-Indians of New England and chewed the resin that formed on spruce trees when the bark was cut. Lumps of spruce for chewing were sold in the eastern United States in the early 1800s making it the first commercial chewing gum in the country.

Modern chewing gum has its origins in the late 1860s with the discovery of *chicle*, a milky substance obtained from the sapodilla tree of the Central American rainforest.

| 8 |

Yet repeated attempts to cultivate sapodilla commercially have failed. As the chewing gum market has grown, synthetic alternatives have had to be developed.

| 9 |

Most alarming is the unpleasant little *chicle* fly that likes to lodge its eggs in the tapper's ears and nose.

Braving these hazards, barefooted and with only a rope and an axe, an experienced *chiclero* will shin a mature tree in minutes to cut a path in the bark for the white sap to flow down to a bag below.

| 10 |

Yet, punishing though this working environment is, the remaining *chicleros* fear for their livelihood.

Not so long ago, the United States alone imported 7,000 tonnes of *chicle* a year from Central America. Last year just 200 tonnes were tapped in the whole of Mexico's Yucatan peninsula. As chewing gum sales have soared, so the manufacturers have turned to synthetics to reduce costs and meet demands.

| 11 |

Plaque acid, which forms when we eat, causes this. Our saliva, which neutralises the acid and supplies minerals such as calcium, phosphate and fluoride, is the body's natural defence. Gum manufacturers say 20 minutes of chewing can increase your salivary flow.

| 12 |

In addition, one hundred and thirty-seven square kilometres of America is devoted entirely to producing the mint that is used in the two most popular chewing gums in the world.

A Gum made from this resulted in a smoother, more satisfying and more elastic chew, and soon a whole industry was born based on this product.

B Meanwhile, the world's gum producers are finding ingenious ways of marketing their products. In addition to all the claims made for gum – it helps you relax, peps you up and eases tension (soldiers during both world wars were regularly supplied with gum) – gum's greatest claim is that it reduces tooth decay.

C Research continues on new textures and flavours. Glycerine and other vegetable oil products are now used to blend the gum base. Most new flavours are artificial – but some flavours still need natural assistance.

D This was not always the case, though. The ancient Greeks chewed a gum-like resin obtained from the bark of the mastic tree, a shrub found mainly in Greece and Turkey. Grecian women, especially, favoured mastic gum to clean their teeth and sweeten their breath.

E Each *chiclero* must carry the liquid on his back to a forest camp, where it is boiled until sticky and made into bricks. Life at the camp is no picnic either, with a monotonous and often deficient maize-based diet washed down by a local drink distilled from sugar cane.

F The *chicleros* grease their hands and arms to prevent the sticky gum sticking to them. The gum is then packed into a wooden mould, pressed down firmly, initialled and dated ready for collection and export.

G Today the few remaining *chicle* gatherers, *chicleros*, eke out a meagre and dangerous living, trekking for miles to tap scattered sapodilla in near-100% humidity. Conditions are appalling: highly poisonous snakes lurk ready to pounce and insects abound.

Part 3

You are going to read a newspaper article about an expedition. For questions **13–19**, choose the answer (**A**, **B**, **C** or **D**) which you think fits best according to the text.

Mark your answers **on the separate answer sheet**.

An awfully big adventure

The Taklamakan Desert in western China is one of the last unexplored places on Earth. It is also one of the most dangerous. Charles Blackmore crossed it, and lived to tell the tale.

There are very few big adventures left and very few heroes. Children's stories used to specialise in them – courageous explorers with sunburnt, leathery skin and eyes narrowed by straining to see into far horizons on their journeys into the unknown. These days you no longer find such people in fiction, let alone in real life. Or so I thought until I met Charles Blackmore.

Blackmore's great adventure consisted of leading an expedition across one of the last unexplored places on earth, the Taklamakan Desert in western China. Its name means 'once entered you never come out', but local people call it the Desert of Death. He recalled the dangers and exhilaration of that amazing trek, in the calm atmosphere of his family home.

The team he led was composed of four Britons (one of them the party's medical officer), an American photographer, four Chinese (all experts on the area), 30 camels and six camel handlers. It later turned out that the camel handlers had never worked with camels before, but were long-distance lorry drivers: a misunderstanding that could have cost everyone their lives and certainly jeopardised the expedition's success. This mixed bunch set out to cross 1,200 kilometres of the world's least hospitable desert and Charles Blackmore has written a mesmerising account of their journey.

At the time, he was about to leave the Army after 14 happy years. He launched the expedition for fun, to fill a gap in his life, to prove something. 'I had always assumed I'd spend my whole life in the Army. I had been offered promotion but suddenly I felt I wanted to see who Charles Blackmore really was, outside all that. It was a tremendous gamble. Tina, my wife, was very worried that I wouldn't come back as nobody had ever done that route; we went into it blind. In the event, it took 59 days to cross from west to east, and the desert was very kind to us.'

Anyone reading his extraordinary account of that crossing will wonder at the use of the word 'kind'. The team suffered unspeakable hardships: dysentery; extremes of temperature; severe thirst and dehydration; the loss of part of their precious water supply. 'But', Blackmore explains, 'when we were at the limits of our own endurance and the camels had gone without water for seven days, we managed to find some. We didn't experience the Taklamakan's legendary sandstorms. And we never hit the raw, biting desert cold that would have totally immobilised us. That's not to say that we weren't fighting against hurdles the whole time. The fine sand got into everything, especially blisters and wounds. The high dunes were torture to climb, for us and for the heavily laden camels, which often rolled over onto us.

'What drove me on more than anything else was the need to survive. We had no contingency plan. Neither our budget nor time allowed one. No aircraft ever flew over us. Once we got into the sandhills we were completely on our own.

'I knew I had the mental stamina for the trip but I was very scared of my physical ability to do it. I remember day one – we sat at the edge of the desert and it was such an inferno that you couldn't breathe. I thought, "We've got to do it now!" At that moment I was a very scared man.'

If it was like that at the beginning, how did they feel towards the end? 'When you've walked for 1,000 kilometres you're not going to duck out. You've endured so much; you've got so much behind you. We were very thin, but very muscular and sinewy despite our physical exhaustion. My body was well-toned and my legs were like pistons. I could walk over anything.'

Midway through the book, Blackmore went on to describe lying in the desert gazing up at a full moon, thinking of his family. How conscious was he of the ordeal it must have been for them? 'Inside me there's someone trying to find peace with himself. When I have doubts about myself now, I go back to the image of the desert and think, well, we managed to pull that together. As a personal achievement, I feel prouder of that expedition than of anything else I've done. Yet in terms of a lifetime's achievement, I think of my family and the happiness we share – against that yardstick, the desert does not measure up, does not compare.'

Has Charles Blackmore found peace? 'I yearn for the challenge – for the open spaces – the resolve of it all. We were buoyed up by the sense of purpose. I find it difficult now to be part of the uniformity of modern life.'

13 Meeting Charles Blackmore changed the writer's opinion about

  A the content of children's fiction.
  B the nature of desert exploration.
  C the existence of traditional heroes.
  D the activities of explorers.

14 When the expedition members set off, some of the group

  A posed an unexpected risk.
  B disagreed with each other.
  C were doubtful of success.
  D went on ahead of the others.

15 Blackmore had decided to set up the expedition because

  A he was certain he could complete it.
  B he wanted to write a book.
  C his aims in life had changed.
  D his self-confidence was low.

16 Which of the following best describes the team's experience of the desert?

  A They were not able to have enough rest.
  B It presented continual difficulties.
  C They sometimes could not make any progress at all.
  D It was worse than they had expected.

17 Which of the following did Blackmore experience during the trip?

  A frustration at the lack of funding
  B regret about the lack of planning
  C realisation that they would receive no help
  D fear that he would let his companions down

18 According to Blackmore, what enabled him to finish the expedition?

  A his strength of will
  B his physical preparation
  C his closeness to his family
  D his understanding of the desert

19 How does Blackmore feel now that the expedition is over?

  A tired but pleased to be home
  B regretful about his family's distress
  C unsure of his ability to repeat it
  D unsettled by the experience

Part 4

You are going to read an article about offices. For questions **20–34**, choose from the offices (**A–D**). The offices may be chosen more than once.

Mark your answers **on the separate answer sheet**.

Of which office is the following stated?

Some of the staff like it and some don't.	20
Advice from an expert has had a good effect.	21
Staff there benefit from the range of work involved.	22
Some members of staff prefer unsuitable furniture.	23
A particular rule has been beneficial.	24
The air quality is better than might be expected.	25
It is often either very hot or very cold.	26
Staff can work in privacy if they want to.	27
There is not enough room for every member of staff to work.	28
It would be better if the furniture were arranged differently.	29
Evidence of the company's achievements is visible.	30
Staff can control the temperature effectively.	31
Staff appear to be under pressure.	32
Working here is like being on display.	33
The staff have made it a pleasant place to work in.	34

IS YOUR OFFICE WORKING OK?

Fresh air and the right chairs are the key to a happy, healthy workforce, according to a new survey. We went to four contrasting offices, to find out how healthy and happy they were as working environments. On our expert panel were a building health consultant; an ergonomist, who studies people's working conditions; and an occupational psychologist. Here are their verdicts.

OFFICE A   ADVERTISING AGENCY

Building Health Consultant: This office is about as simple as it could possibly be; no central heating, no mechanical ventilation, windows opening straight onto the street. It is difficult to see why this space works but the occupants, who are part of a small, dynamic team, appear to have few complaints. They adapt to the changing seasons by opening doors and roof panels or switching on electric radiators – pretty much, perhaps, as they do in their own homes. This may be the key: a team of seven people have created a happy, homely working environment and do not have to put up with any externally imposed bureaucracy.

Ergonomist: The furniture here has evolved; no two pieces match. Much of it actually creates bad working postures. Chairs are old, most aren't adjustable and many are broken. Although in that way this environment is poor, the personnel have a varied work schedule, which they control – office work, out meeting clients, making presentations, and so on. This variety reduces the risk of fatigue, boredom or muscular problems.

Occupational Psychologist: Staff are delighted with the variety of work and the versatility of the office space. They said their office was 'just the right size' – small enough to know what colleagues were doing, large enough to be able to be on your own and focus on personal work. I found the office attractive and fun, simultaneously conveying images of efficiency and creativity.

OFFICE B   NEWS SERVICE

Building Health Consultant: While the office may not be very exciting, it appears comfortable and is not disliked by the staff. The air quality and general maintenance standards appear to be good. A 'Recycle Waste Paper' policy has been received favourably by staff and has led to a greater interest in recycling in general.

Ergonomist: I was not surprised to learn that the company had already employed the services of an ergonomist. Chairs are excellent, lighting and computer equipment are good. Space provision is good, although the layout could be improved. But the environment is impersonal and unstimulating, with grey, bare walls.

Occupational Psychologist: Walls are bare apart from year planners and a poster describing maternity rights. Most staff have been there for at least five years and relationships are satisfactory. The office could be improved if desks were positioned to make the sharing of information easier. Proof of success or information on forthcoming projects could be displayed on the walls.

OFFICE C   BANK

Building Health Consultant: An office that produces mixed reactions from those working in it. The feeling inside is akin to being in a glass case, viewed by, and viewing, countless similar exhibits. Despite relatively small space, the air did not appear to be stale due to effective air-conditioning.

Ergonomist: The office area is, sadly, very standard and totally uninspiring. The desks are adequate, but only just. Not all the chairs being used for computer operation conform to requirements but this is user choice. Computer screens are often on small desk units with lowered keyboard shelves; this is no longer considered appropriate for modern equipment.

Occupational Psychologist: Staff are mutually supportive and well served by technology. Numerous communications awards are on display. The wood coloured panelling and brown carpet give a slightly sombre effect. The office is a buzz of activity.

OFFICE D   NEWSPAPER

Building Health Consultant: It is difficult to say anything good about this building. The air-conditioning control is very crude, resulting in large variations in temperature. The space is cluttered and most people have inadequate desk space. The office is very dusty – there are plenty of places for dust to lodge. The shed-type roof also collects dust, which, if disturbed, showers those sitting below.

Ergonomist: The furniture would be more at home in a carpentry workshop than in a high-tech industry. Most of the chairs are of little value to keyboard users, particularly those who are shorter than about 1.75 m. Many chairs are old, lack suitable adjustment and have armrests that prevent the user from getting sufficiently close to the desk.

Occupational Psychologist: Old brown chairs, soiled carpets, dust and dirt everywhere. A lot of scope for improvement – the place needs a good tidy-up, individual success could be more recognised and the air conditioning needs to be improved immediately. Few conversations were going on when we visited; everybody seemed stressed and driven by deadlines. The company needs to adopt a policy of team-working.

Test 2

PAPER 2 WRITING (1 hour 30 minutes)

Part 1

You **must** answer this question. Write your answer in **180–220** words in an appropriate style.

1 You and a friend, Sam, bought some CDs to help you improve your English. You were not happy with the CDs and have decided to write to the publisher, CD World.

Read the email from Sam and the advertisement for the CDs below, on which you have made some notes. Then, **using the information appropriately**, write a letter to CD World explaining why you bought the CDs, why you are dissatisfied and saying what you would like the company to do.

From: sam@rds.ac.uk
Subject: CDs!

How did you get on with the language practice CDs? I wasn't very impressed. "English conversation in a week" – I don't think so! The ad was dishonest – I think we should try to get our money back.

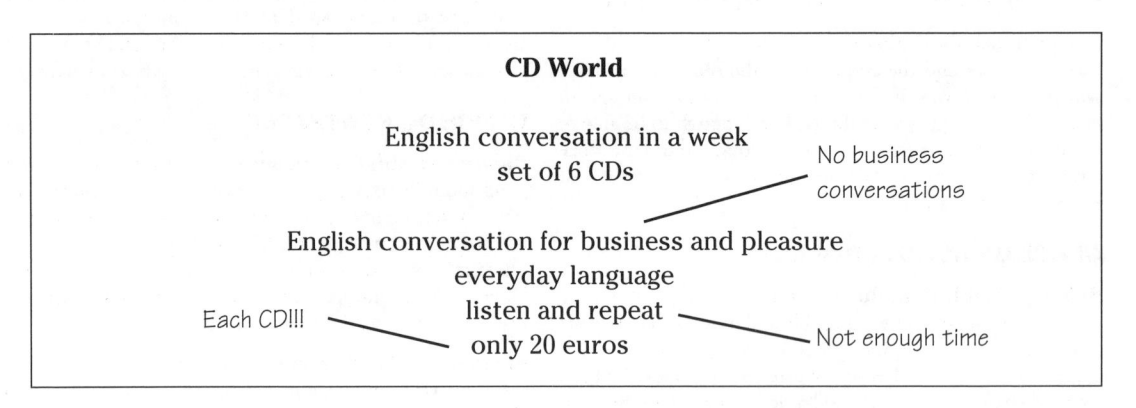

CD World

English conversation in a week
set of 6 CDs — *No business conversations*

English conversation for business and pleasure
everyday language
listen and repeat
only 20 euros

Each CD!!!

Not enough time

Now write your **letter** to CD World, as outlined above. You should use your own words as far as possible. You do not need to include the address or the date.

Paper 2 Writing

Part 2

Choose **one** of the following writing tasks. Your answer should follow exactly the instructions given. Write approximately **220–260** words.

2   You would like to start a monthly magazine in English for students at the college where you are studying. You have decided to send a proposal to the college Principal asking for permission and financial support. Your proposal must include the following:
   - why you want to start the magazine
   - what the first issue would include
   - what support and financial help you need from the college.

   Write your **proposal**.

3   While staying in an international youth hostel, you see the following announcement in its magazine:

   > **COMPETITION**
   > Should we travel alone, with friends or with family?
   > What are the benefits of each and are there any disadvantages?
   > Write and tell us what you think.
   > We will publish the best entries in next month's magazine and the winner will receive a mountain bike.

   Write your **competition entry**.

4   An English magazine has a weekly column called *It'll Cost The Earth*. As part of their worldwide investigation into environmental issues, they have asked you to write a report for them, addressing the following questions:
   - What is being done to cut down on the use of energy and natural resources in your village, town or city?
   - How successful are these measures?
   - What more could be done?

   Write your **report**.

5   Answer **one** of the following two questions based on **one** of the titles below.

   (a)   Adriana Trigiani: *Big Stone Gap*

   You have decided to write an article on *Big Stone Gap* for your college magazine. Your article should focus on the character of Ave Maria and her relationships with two of the other characters in the story. You should explain why you find these two relationships interesting and should discuss which of these two relationships is more important to Ave Maria.

   Write your **article**.

   (b)   Dick Francis: *In the Frame*

   Your teacher has asked you to write an essay on *In the Frame*. Your essay should briefly describe the beginning and the ending of the story and you should explain how effective you think each of these parts of the story is.

   Write your **essay**.

Test 2

PAPER 3   USE OF ENGLISH (1 hour)

Part 1

For questions **1–12**, read the text below and decide which answer (**A**, **B**, **C** or **D**) best fits each gap. There is an example at the beginning (**0**).

Mark your answers **on the separate answer sheet**.

Example:

0 A turn   **B** arrival   **C** origin   **D** introduction

| 0 | A | B | C | D |

Sports photography

Sport as a spectacle and photography as a way of recording action have developed together. At the **(0)** ..... of the 20th century, Edward Muybridge was experimenting with photographs of movement. His pictures of a runner **(1)** ..... in every history of photography. Another milestone was when the scientist and photographer Harold Edgerton **(2)** ..... the limits of photographic technology with his study of a **(3)** ..... of milk hitting the surface of a dish. Another advance was the development of miniature cameras in the late 1920s, which made it possible for sports photographers to **(4)** ..... their cumbersome cameras behind.

The arrival of television was a significant development in the transmission of sport. Paradoxically, it was of benefit to still photographers. People who watched a sports event on TV, with all its movement and action, **(5)** ..... the still image as a reminder of the game.

Looking back, we can see how **(6)** ..... sports photography has changed. **(7)** ..... sports photographers were as interested in the stories behind the sport as in the sport itself. Contemporary sports photography **(8)** ..... the glamour of sport, the colour and the action. But the best sports photographers today do more than **(9)** ..... tell the story of the event, or make a **(10)** ..... of it. They **(11)** ..... in a single dramatic moment the real emotions of the participants, emotions with which people looking at the photographs can **(12)** ..... .

1	**A** exhibit	**B** show	**C** feature	**D** demonstrate
2	**A** enlarged	**B** extended	**C** prolonged	**D** spread
3	**A** splash	**B** drop	**C** dash	**D** drip
4	**A** put	**B** keep	**C** lay	**D** leave
5	**A** chose	**B** valued	**C** pointed	**D** cheered
6	**A** highly	**B** radically	**C** extremely	**D** severely
7	**A** Initial	**B** First	**C** Early	**D** Primary
8	**A** outlines	**B** signals	**C** emphasises	**D** forms
9	**A** simply	**B** alone	**C** singly	**D** only
10	**A** preservation	**B** store	**C** mark	**D** record
11	**A** seize	**B** grasp	**C** capture	**D** secure
12	**A** identify	**B** share	**C** unite	**D** join

Part 2

For questions **13–27**, read the text below and think of the word which best fits each gap. Use only **one** word in each gap. There is an example at the beginning (**0**).

Write your answer in **CAPITAL LETTERS on the separate answer sheet**.

Example: | 0 | W | H | A | T | | | | | | | | | | | |

Traffic jams are nothing new

In the age before the motor car, (**0**) ..... was travelling in London like? Photographs taken 100 years ago showing packed streets indicate that it was much the (**13**) ..... as it is now. It has (**14**) ..... calculated that, even with new anti-congestion systems in place, commuters who choose the car to get to work travel at (**15**) ..... average speed of 17 kph from their homes (**16**) ..... the suburbs to offices in the centre. (**17**) ..... is virtually the same speed that they (**18**) ..... have travelled at in a horse and carriage a century ago.

As towns and cities grow, (**19**) ..... does traffic, whether in the form of the horse and carriage (**20**) ..... the modern motor car. It would seem that, wherever (**21**) ..... are people who need to go somewhere, they would (**22**) ..... be carried than walk or pedal. The photographs show that, in terms (**23**) ..... congestion and speed, traffic in London hasn't changed over the past 100 years. London has had traffic jams ever (**24**) ..... it became a huge city. It is only the vehicles that have changed.

However, apart (**25**) ..... the congestion which affected London long (**26**) ..... the car came along, the age of the horse produced relatively (**27**) ..... unpleasantness. This age, for example, saw none of the exhaust fumes which city dwellers have to live with today.

Part 3

For questions **28–37**, read the text below. Use the word given in capitals at the end of some of the lines to form a word that fits in the gap **in the same line**. There is an example at the beginning (**0**).

Write your answers **IN CAPITAL LETTERS on the separate answer sheet**.

Example: | 0 | C | O | M | P | A | N | I | O | N | S | | | | | |

A Mexican cookery course

On holiday last year my two travelling (0) ..... and I joined a day's   **COMPANY**

cookery course in a Mexican restaurant. There were eight (28) ..... ,   **PARTICIPATE**

all keen to learn the secrets of the nation's cuisine. The students ranged

from people who already had some (29) ..... in the kitchen, to totally   **EXPERT**

(30) ..... people like myself.   **SKILL**

Our teacher, Liana Cabrera, started with a short talk, then handed out some

notes giving (31) ..... of terms we'd be coming across. Soon we were   **EXPLAIN**

trying out a range of exotic ingredients, with (32) ..... good results. Cabrera   **SURPRISE**

started giving cookery lessons five years ago, and has become quite a

(33) ..... , with long waiting lists for her courses. And because of her   **CELEBRATE**

extensive knowledge of almost-forgotten regional dishes she is also a

regular (34) ..... to cookery programmes on national television.   **CONTRIBUTE**

In the afternoon I joined the salsa-making team, with rather (35) ..... results.   **DISASTER**

My colleagues complained that my food was so (36) ..... hot it made their   **PAIN**

eyes water. Their own efforts turned out (37) ..... better than mine.   **CONSIDER**

The communal meal at the end of the day was delicious, and I'd not only

learnt something about cooking, but I'd also broadened my understanding

of Mexican culture.

Test 2

Part 4

For questions **38–42**, think of **one** word only which can be used appropriately in all three sentences. Here is an example (**0**).

Example:

0 The committee decided to .... the money equally between the two charities.

I can't believe that John and Maggie have decided to .... up after 20 years of marriage.

To serve a watermelon you need to .... it down the centre with a sharp knife.

Example: | 0 | S | P | L | I | T | | | | | | | | | |

Write **only** the missing word **IN CAPITAL LETTERS on the separate answer sheet**.

---

38 Are you .... to go out with us tonight, or are you working overtime as usual?

My brother's very .... with his advice, which can be quite annoying.

This .... offer ends next week, so be sure to get down to the store and take advantage of it – it's your last chance.

39 My previous neighbour always .... that she knew a lot of famous actors, but I'm not sure it was true.

After the business trip, John made sure he .... his expenses promptly.

Loss of habitat and damage to the environment has .... the lives of many animals.

40 She wasn't concentrating properly and did her homework ....

He reacted .... to the injection and felt sick all day.

I .... need some sleep; I'm exhausted after that long drive.

41 Amy is by .... rather a shy person.

Generally, the .... of a shop's response should depend on the seriousness of a customer's complaint.

Eric always had a keen love of .... , so I'm not surprised that he has chosen an outdoor job.

42 Felicity .... great insight into the music business during her period of work experience at the record company.

The intruder .... access to the building through a skylight which had been left open.

Greg was horrified to find that after two weeks on his special diet he had actually .... weight.

Test 2

Part 5

For questions **43–50**, complete the second sentence so that it has a similar meaning to the first sentence, using the word given. **Do not change the word given**. You must use between **three** and **six** words, including the word given. Here is an example (**0**).

Example:

0 Fernanda refused to wear her sister's old dress.

   NOT

   Fernanda said that ………………………………………………… her sister's old dress.

The gap can be filled with the words 'she would not wear', so you write:

Example: | 0 | SHE WOULD NOT WEAR |

Write the missing words **IN CAPITAL LETTERS** on the separate answer sheet.

---

43 There is no way Lisa will give up her independence to get married.

   OF

   Lisa has ………………………………………………… up her independence to get married.

44 Simon really ought to make a decision about his future.

   MIND

   It's high time Simon ………………………………………………… about his future.

45 Pay claims must be submitted before the end of the month.

   PUT

   You have ………………………………………………… your pay claims before the end of the month.

46 There are various ways of avoiding insect bites.

   PREVENTED

   Insect bites can ………………………………………………… various ways.

47 I think learning to use a typewriter is a waste of time.

   POINT

   I can't ………………………………………………… how to use a typewriter.

48 Your mobile phone should be switched off at all times during the performance.

   SHOULD

   Under no ………………………………………………… your mobile phone switched on during the performance.

49 If you don't pay on time, your booking will be cancelled.

   RESULT

   Failure to ………………………………………………… your booking being cancelled.

50 Darius soon recovered after the operation on his knee and was able to rejoin the team.

   MADE

   After the operation on his knee, Darius ………………………………………………… and was able to rejoin the team.

Test 2

PAPER 4 LISTENING (approximately 40 minutes)

Part 1

You will hear three different extracts. For questions **1–6**, choose the answer (**A**, **B** or **C**) which fits best according to what you hear. There are two questions for each extract.

Extract One

You overhear part of a conversation between the secretary of a golf club and a visitor to the club.

1   What does the visitor feel about installing satellite navigation in her car?

   A   worried about its cost

   B   unsure of its usefulness

   C   doubtful about its reliability

2   When he talks about in-car satellite navigation systems, the secretary is

   A   helping his visitor to choose the best model.

   B   providing his visitor with information about them.

   C   warning his visitor about the drawbacks of using one.

Extract Two

You hear part of a discussion in which the anthropologist Paula Drew and the comedian Mike Morton are talking about their lives.

3   What does Mike say about his use of comedy as a child?

   A   He appeared to have an instinctive talent for it.

   B   His long-term friendships depended on it.

   C   It was one of a number of skills he developed.

4   Both speakers agree that, for a successful life, people need

   A   a belief in themselves.

   B   a clearly defined goal.

   C   a commitment to hard work.

52

Paper 4 Listening

Extract Three

You hear part of a radio discussion about holiday reading.

5   The man reads books which

　　A   remind him of people he's met.

　　B   make a change from his work.

　　C   are set somewhere he doesn't know.

6   His work involves

　　A   a lot of travel.

　　B   looking out for new words.

　　C   studying classical literature.

Test 2

Part 2

You will hear a reporter called Ruth Sampson describing a visit she made to the Arctic Circle with a team of Canadian wildlife experts. For questions **7–14**, complete the sentences.

A visit to the Arctic Circle

As her plane was landing, [_____ **7** _____] were the first animals Ruth saw.

Soon after arriving, the team of biologists was able to identify a [_____ **8** _____] in the distance.

The term [_____ **9** _____] is used to describe a small patch of ground where the growth of plants is possible.

The largest part of the yellow Arctic poppy is its [_____ **10** _____].

The majority of birds returning to the area in the spring feed on [_____ **11** _____].

The team stayed in tents with small [_____ **12** _____] at the entrance.

Ruth was given advice on what to do if approached by a [_____ **13** _____].

It was difficult for Ruth to carry out her work because [_____ **14** _____] are affected by freezing temperatures.

Paper 4 Listening

Part 3

You will hear a radio interview with the gardening experts Jed and Helena Stone. For questions **15–20**, choose the answer (**A**, **B**, **C** or **D**) which fits best according to what you hear.

15 How does Helena feel about the use of Jed's name for their joint business?

   A   occasionally frustrated that her contribution goes unnoticed
   B   amused that they have a name people tend to remember
   C   appreciative of the respect that the name has brought her
   D   irritated by the fact that Jed is more of a celebrity than she is

16 What is Jed's attitude to his public profile?

   A   He likes the fact that complete strangers often want to talk to him.
   B   He's unhappy that it prevents him doing everyday activities.
   C   He enjoys it more now than he did when he was younger.
   D   He's proud of the way it reflects his achievements.

17 How did Helena feel about her work on *The Travel Show*?

   A   She would have enjoyed it more in different circumstances.
   B   It was convenient for her to be away from the house then.
   C   It was a welcome alternative to manual work.
   D   She felt obliged to do it at that particular time.

18 What gave Jed the incentive to make a jewel garden?

   A   He wanted to realise a long-held ambition.
   B   He had led people to believe that it already existed.
   C   He wanted to show pictures of it at a gardening event.
   D   He was inspired by the illustrations at a talk he attended.

19 What explanation does Helena give for the name of the garden?

   A   It provided a useful framework for the project.
   B   It was a response to the bright colours they wanted there.
   C   It allowed them to experiment with a wide range of options.
   D   It was meant to inspire them to embrace unconventional ideas.

20 Jed says that, for him, the name 'jewel garden' is

   A   a reminder of the value of creativity.
   B   an appropriate one for something so beautiful.
   C   a positive way of combining both past and present.
   D   a way of explaining his philosophy of design to people.

Part 4

You will hear five short extracts in which people are talking about weekend activities.

TASK ONE

For questions **21–25**, choose from the list **A–H** the activity each speaker is describing.

TASK TWO

For questions **26–30**, choose from the list **A–H** what each speaker felt about their activity.

While you listen you must complete both tasks.

A mountaineering

B going to the theatre

C swimming in a lake

D dining in a restaurant

E watching a football match

F fishing in a river

G wandering around a market

H attending a wedding

Speaker 1 — 21
Speaker 2 — 22
Speaker 3 — 23
Speaker 4 — 24
Speaker 5 — 25

A It was disappointing.

B It was confusing.

C It was uneventful.

D It was overcrowded.

E It was frightening.

F It was unusual.

G It was amusing.

H It was exhausting.

Speaker 1 — 26
Speaker 2 — 27
Speaker 3 — 28
Speaker 4 — 29
Speaker 5 — 30

PAPER 5 SPEAKING (15 minutes)

There are two examiners. One (the interlocutor) conducts the test, providing you with the necessary materials and explaining what you have to do. The other examiner (the assessor) is introduced to you, but then takes no further part in the interaction.

Part 1 (3 minutes)

The interlocutor first asks you and your partner a few questions. The interlocutor asks candidates for some information about themselves, then widens the scope of the questions by asking about, e.g. candidates' leisure activities, studies, travel and daily life. Candidates are expected to respond to the interlocutor's and listen to what their partner has to say.

Part 2 (a one-minute long turn for each candidate, plus 30-second response from the second candidate)

You are each given the opportunity to talk for about a minute, and to comment briefly after your partner has spoken.
   The interlocutor gives you a set of pictures and asks you to talk about them for about one minute. It is important to listen carefully to the interlocutor's instructions. The interlocutor then asks your partner a question about your pictures and your partner responds briefly.
   You are then given another set of pictures to look at. Your partner talks about these pictures for about one minute. This time the interlocutor asks you a question about your partner's pictures and you respond briefly.

Part 3 (approximately 4 minutes)

In this part of the test you and your partner are asked to talk together. The interlocutor places a new set of pictures on the table between you. This stimulus provides the basis for a discussion. The interlocutor explains what you have to do.

Part 4 (approximately 4 minutes)

The interlocutor asks some further questions, which leads to a more general discussion of what you have talked about in Part 3. You may comment on your partner's answers if you wish.

Test 3

PAPER 1 READING (1 hour 15 minutes)

Part 1

You are going to read three extracts which are all concerned in some way with making decisions. For questions **1–6**, choose the answer (**A**, **B**, **C** or **D**) which you think fits best according to the text.

Mark your answers **on the separate answer sheet**.

Decision making in business: Gordon Bethune

Having decided that Continental Airlines was worth saving, the question for Gordon Bethune – brought in to rescue the struggling company in 1994 – was how to do it. He and consultant Greg Brenneman mapped out a turnaround strategy.

In retrospect their plan seems commonsensical and obvious, but at the time the opposite appeared closer to the truth, for two reasons. First, the company was in the midst of a crisis. (At one of its darkest moments, it was less than six weeks away from not having enough cash to meet the payroll.) And the second point is this: straightforward as the strategy might have been, no one had ever come up with, nor implemented, such a plan. (The airline had gone through 10 presidents in 10 years.)

'The first step was to figure out exactly what we wanted to do,' Bethune says. 'We needed to develop a simple clear strategy, one that everyone could understand, and once it was in place, one that we weren't going to deviate from.'

Easier said than done. When you are in the middle of an emergency – and trying to save an airline that is desperately short of cash certainly qualified as an emergency – there is a natural tendency to grasp at straws, to go after whatever will bring in money to keep you solvent for another week or two. Bethune understood the temptation and fought it off.

1   The writer believes that when Bethune and Brenneman produced their plan,

   A it seemed unlikely to achieve its objectives.
   B it was the best way to raise money quickly.
   C it was likely to cost too much to implement.
   D it seemed too similar to previous strategies.

2   What does the writer imply about Bethune?

   A He understood the importance of being flexible.
   B He had considerable experience of dealing with crises.
   C He faced opposition from within the company.
   D He took a long-term view of the situation.

59

Extract from a novel

Children's toys

Left to himself, Eustace fell into a day-dream. He thought of his toys and tried to decide which of them he should give to his sister Barbara; he had been told he must part with some of them, and indeed it would not make much difference if they were hers by right, since she already treated them as such. Whenever he went to take them from her she resisted with loud screams. Eustace realised that she wanted them but he did not think she ought to have them. She could not use them intelligently, and besides, they belonged to him. He might be too old to play with them but they brought back the past in a way that nothing else did. Certain moments in the past were like buried treasure to Eustace, living relics of a golden age which it was an ecstasy to contemplate. His toys put him in touch with these secret jewels of experience; they could not perform the miracle if they belonged to someone else. But on the single occasion when he had asserted his ownership and removed the toy rabbit from Barbara, who was sucking its ears, nearly everyone had been against him and there was a terrible scene.

3   In this extract the writer focuses on Eustace's

   A   desire to improve his relationship with his sister.
   B   efforts to find a solution to a dilemma.
   C   wish to increase the number of his possessions.
   D   sense of being different from other people.

4   Eustace liked his toys because of

   A   incidents associated with them.
   B   the people who had given them to him.
   C   what he could do with them.
   D   their rare and valuable nature.

Children's involvement in family decision making

In Britain, as children's rights to citizenship have strengthened over recent years, a strong presumption in favour of involving children in decisions on matters that directly affect them has developed in a number of areas of law, public policy and professional practice (for example, school councils). Yet surprisingly little is known about how far children's participation extends to their home lives and the routine business of everyday life. A recent study, based on group discussions and in-depth interviews with 117 children aged between eight and ten, examined how and to what extent the children were involved in shaping their own and their families' domestic lives.

Many of the findings were illuminating. The ways in which families made decisions involved a subtle, complex and dynamic set of processes in which children could exert a decisive influence. Most families operated democratically but children accepted the ultimate authority of their parents, provided that they felt their parents acted 'fairly'. For children, 'fairness' had more to do with being treated equitably than simply having the decision made in their favour. Children could use claims to fairness as a moral lever in negotiations with parents. Family precedent, especially that set by older brothers and sisters, was an influential factor in 'good decision making' and was a more common point of reference than the experience of peers and other families.

5   In the first paragraph, the writer implies that

   A   the involvement of children is damaging the quality of public decision making.
   B   greater understanding of domestic decision making involving children would be beneficial.
   C   children would make better decisions if they understood the decision-making process better.
   D   children are keen to become more involved in domestic decision making.

6   According to the second paragraph, children tended to accept decisions that

   A   were similar to decisions made by other families.
   B   were made in a way that conformed with their sense of justice.
   C   were more favourable to them than to their brothers and sisters.
   D   were made by giving the child as much authority as their parents.

Part 2

You are going to read an extract from a newspaper article about working from home. Six paragraphs have been removed from the extract. Choose from the paragraphs **A–G** the one which fits each gap (**7–12**). There is one extra paragraph which you do not need to use.

Mark your answers **on the separate answer sheet**.

Plugging in the home

Georgina McGuiness had taken a long career break from journalism and she felt out of touch with the changes brought about by technology. She recounts here how she was able to transform the family home into an efficient workplace.

Last year I turned 37 and realised that time was running out if I wanted to resurrect a career in journalism.

A quick glance at my curriculum vitae showed that I was shamefully stuck in the 1980s, when a piece of carbon wedged in between several sheets of paper in a typewriter was the state of the art. It seemed that only a madman would let me loose on a computer in his newsroom. And why did most of the jobs advertised ask for experience in desktop publishing – which I didn't have?

| 7 | |

Clearly, there was a gaping hole in what was left of my career and I had to act quickly. Leaving home before the children did would be fraught with obstacles, or so I thought until I entered a competition in a local newspaper. Like a success story you read or hear about that only ever happens to other people, my family and I won a computer package.

| 8 | |

I had everything I would need for working from home – and I could still manage to take the children to school. They were confident with computers from the start, already well versed in them from school. I was much more hesitant, convinced that all my work would disappear without trace if I pressed the wrong button. I could not have been more wrong.

| 9 | |

I recently began freelancing for a magazine, contributing about two articles a month, and I have become smug in the knowledge that I have the best of two worlds.

So how has the computer helped me? Since my schooldays I have always worked at a desk that can only be described as a chaotic mess.

| 10 | |

Spreadsheets help keep a record of income and expenses and the Internet means I can research stories, ask for further information on the bulletin board in the journalism or publishing forums and even discuss the pros and cons of working from home with people from all over the world.

| 11 | |

However, there is a growing band of people who have recently bought multi-media PCs, not just for the educational, leisure and entertainment facilities. In my street alone there appears to be a cottage industry evolving from the sheer convenience of not having to join the commuter struggle into the city each day. So what characterises modern-day home workers?

| 12 | |

Taking this into account, I seem to fit in well. And who knows, one day I will be emailing a column to a newspaper in Melbourne or, better still, publishing my own magazine from home. It seems the sky, or should I say cyberspace, is the limit.

A Consequently, I was always losing scraps of paper containing vital bits of information. The computer has transformed me into an organised worker, particularly when it comes to office administration.

B If all this sounds too good to be true, there is a dark side to computing from home. You can be in isolation from physical human contact and also there are the distractions of putting urgent jobs about the house first.

C To get an idea of the speed and convenience with which someone based at home can send their work back to the office, this article will be sent in a matter of minutes via a modem straight into the editor's computer.

D I thought I had a better chance of hosting a seminar in nuclear physics than attempting to lay out a page on a computer. I was the family technophobe; even pocket calculators were a mystery to me and I still don't know how to use the timer on the DVD.

E A recent report was unable to give an exact profile. Home-office workers comprise both males and females, aged between 25 and 55. However, they are usually well educated and more likely to be working in sales, marketing or technology.

F Though far from being adroit, I did manage to learn the basic skills I needed – it was all so logical, easy and idiot-proof. And, like everything that you persevere with, you learn a little more each day.

G Supplied with a laptop computer to free my husband from his desk, and a personal computer for us all, we dived in at the deep end. The children forsook the television and I set up a mini-office in a corner of the kitchen with my computer linking me to the information superhighway.

Part 3

You are going to read a newspaper article. For questions **13–19**, choose the answer (**A**, **B**, **C** or **D**) which you think fits best according to the text. Mark your answers **on the separate answer sheet**.

Solar Survivor

Charles Clover ventures inside Britain's most environmentally friendly home.

Southwell in Nottinghamshire is full of surprises. The first is Britain's least-known ancient cathedral, Southwell Minster, celebrated by writers of an environmental disposition for the pagan figures of 'green' men which medieval craftsmen carved into the decorations in its thirteenth-century chapter house. The second, appropriately enough, is Britain's greenest dwelling, the 'autonomous house', designed and built by Robert and Brenda Vale.

The Vales use rainwater for washing and drinking, recycle their sewage into garden compost and heat their house with waste heat from electrical appliances and their own body heat, together with that of their three teenage children and their two cats, Edison and Faraday. You could easily miss the traditional-looking house, roofed with clay pantiles, on a verdant corner plot 300 metres from the Minster. It was designed to echo the burnt-orange brick of the town's nineteenth-century buildings and won approval from the planners even though it is in a conservation area.

Ring the solar-powered doorbell and there is total silence. The house is super-insulated, with krypton-filled triple-glazed windows, which means that you do not hear a sound inside. Once inside and with your shoes off (at Robert's insistence), there is a monastic stillness. It is a sunny summer's day, the windows are closed and the conservatory is doing its normal job of warming the air before it ventilates the house. Vale apologises and moves through the house, opening ingenious ventilation shafts and windows. You need to create draughts because draught-proofing is everywhere: even Edison and Faraday have their own air-locked miniature door.

The Vales, who teach architecture at Nottingham University, were serious about the environment long before it hit the political agenda. They wrote a book on green architecture back in the 1970s, *The Autonomous House*. They began by designing a building which emitted no carbon dioxide. Then they got carried away and decided to do without mains water as well. They designed composting earth closets, lowered rainwater tanks into the cellar, and specified copper gutters to protect the drinking water, which they pass through two filters before use. Water from washing runs into the garden (the Vales don't have a dishwasher because they believe it is morally unacceptable to use strong detergents). Most details have a similar statement in mind.

'We wanted people to see that it was possible to design a house which would be far less detrimental to the environment, without having to live in the dark,' says Robert. 'It would not be medieval.' The house's only medieval aspect is aesthetic: the hall, which includes the hearth and the staircase, rises the full height of the building.

The Vales pay no water bills. And last winter the house used only nine units of electricity a day costing about 70p – which is roughly what other four-bedroomed houses use on top of heating. Soon it will use even less, when £20,000 worth of solar water heating panels and generating equipment arrive and are erected in the garden. The house will draw electricity from the mains supply for cooking and running the appliances, but will generate a surplus of electricity. There will even be enough, one day, to charge an electric car. The only heating is a small wood-burning stove in the hall, which the Vales claim not to use except in the very coldest weather.

So is it warm in winter? One night in February when I happened to call on him, Robert was sitting reading. It was too warm to light the fire, he said. The room temperature on the first floor was 18°C, less than the generally expected temperature of living areas, but entirely comfortable, he claimed, because there are no draughts, no radiant heat loss, since everything you touch is at the same temperature. Perceived temperature depends on these factors. An Edwardian lady in the early years of the twentieth century was entirely comfortable at 12.5°C, he says, because of the insulation provided by her clothing. Those people who live in pre-1900 housing, he suggests, should simply go back to living as people did then. Somehow, it is difficult to think of this idea catching on.

The house's secret is that it is low-tech and there is little to go wrong. Almost everything was obtained from a builder's merchant and installed by local craftsmen. This made the house cheap to build – it cost the same price per square metre as low-cost housing for rent. Not surprisingly, the commercial building companies are determinedly resisting this idea.

Paper 1 Reading

13 According to the writer, the exterior of the Vales' house is

   A unique.
   B unattractive.
   C controversial.
   D unremarkable.

14 Why did Robert Vale apologise to the writer on his arrival?

   A The ventilation system had failed.
   B The temperature was uncomfortable.
   C The conservatory was not functioning properly.
   D The draughts were unwelcome.

15 What does the writer suggest about environmental issues in the fourth paragraph?

   A They have always been a difficult topic.
   B They have become a subject of political debate.
   C The Vales have changed their views in recent years.
   D The Vales have begun to take a political interest in the subject.

16 What does the writer imply about the decision not to use mains water in the Vales' house?

   A It was impractical.
   B It was later regretted.
   C It was an extreme choice.
   D It caused unexpected problems.

17 In Robert Vale's opinion, his home challenges the idea that houses designed with the environment in mind must be

   A draughty.
   B primitive.
   C small.
   D ugly.

18 The planned changes to the house's electrical system will mean that

   A the house will produce more electricity than it uses.
   B the Vales will not use electricity from the mains supply.
   C the house will use more electricity than it does now.
   D the Vales' electricity bills will remain at their current level.

19 According to Robert Vale, the house was comfortable in February because

   A no variations in temperature could be noticed.
   B 18°C was acceptable for ordinary houses.
   C it was not a particularly cold winter.
   D he had got used to the temperature.

65

Test 3

Part 4

You are going to read an article about books. For questions **20–34**, choose from the publishers (**A–E**). The publishers may be chosen more than once.

Mark your answers **on the separate answer sheet**.

Which publisher(s)

say that some books succeed whether they are reviewed or not?	20	21
mentions reviewers taking the opportunity to display their own expertise?	22	
describes how good reviews can contribute to the commercial failure of a book?	23	
says that writers and publishers do not react to negative reviews in the same way?	24	
feels that certain books are frequently overlooked by reviewers?	25	
talks about the sales of some books being stimulated by mixed reviews?	26	
suggest that the length of a review may be more important to publishers than what it actually says?	27	28
refer to the influence of reviews written by well-known people?	29	30
says the effect of reviews on sales does not have a regular pattern?	31	
mention reviews being a crucial form of promotion?	32	33
believes there has been an improvement in the standard of book reviews?	34	

DO REVIEWS SELL BOOKS?

We asked five leading British publishers about the effect of the reviews of a book on its commercial success. Here is what they said.

Publisher A

Reviews are absolutely key for publishers – the first part of the newspaper we turn to. The Book Marketing Council found some years ago that when questioned on why they had bought a particular book, more people cited reviews than any other prompting influence (advertisements, word of mouth, bookshop display, etc.).

Authors' responses to reviews are slightly different from publishers'. Both are devastated by no reviews, but publishers are usually more equable about the bad reviews, judging that column inches are what matter and that a combination of denunciation and ecstatic praise can actually create sales as readers decide to judge for themselves.

Publishers probably get the most pleasure from a review which precisely echoes their own response to a book – they are often the first 'reader'.

Publisher B

While publishers and the press fairly obviously have a common interest in the nature of book review pages, one also needs to remember that their requirements substantially differ: a newspaper or magazine needs to provide its readers with appropriately entertaining material; a publishing house wants to see books, preferably its own, reviewed, preferably favourably.

Without any question, book reviewing is 'better' – more diverse, less elitist – than 40 years ago, when I began reading review pages. That said, there is still a long-grumbled-about tendency to neglect the book medium read by a majority – namely paperbacks. The weekly roundups aren't really adequate even if conscientiously done. And even original paperbacks only rarely receive serious coverage.

But publishers shouldn't complain too much. Reviews are an economical way of getting a book and an author known. There is no question that a lively account of a new book by a trusted name can generate sales – even more if there are several of them.

Publisher C

Reviews are the oxygen of literary publishing; without them, we would be cut off from an essential life-source. Because the books we publish are generally not by 'brand-name' authors, whose books sell with or without reviews, and because we seldom advertise, we depend on the space given to our books by literary editors.

When the reviews are favourable, of course, they are worth infinitely more than any advertisement. The reader knows that the good review is not influenced by the publisher's marketing budget: it is the voice of reason, and there is no doubt that it helps to sell books. Publishers themselves often claim that they look for size rather than content in reviews.

The actual effect of reviews on sales is the inscrutable heart of the whole business. Good reviews can launch a book and a career and occasionally lift sales into the stratosphere: but never entirely on their own. There has to be some fusion with other elements – a word-of-mouth network of recommendation, a robust response from the book trade, clever marketing.

Publisher D

The relationship in Britain between publishing and reviewing? I wish I knew! In the United States it's simple: the *New York Times* can make or break a book with a single review. Here, though, the people in the bookshops often don't appear to take much notice of them.

It sometimes takes 20 years of consistently outstanding reviews for people to start reading a good writer's work. Yet some of the most dismally received books, or books not yet reviewed, are the biggest sellers of all. So it's all very unpredictable, though non-fiction is less so.

Mind you, non-fiction does allow reviewers to indulge themselves by telling us what they know about the subject of the book under review rather than about the book itself.

Publisher E

Of course, all publishers and all writers dream of long, uniformly laudatory reviews. But do they sell books? I once published a biography. The reviews were everything I could have craved. The book was a flop – because everyone thought that, by reading the lengthy reviews, they need not buy the book.

Does the name of the reviewer make a difference? Thirty years ago, if certain reviewers praised a book, the public seemed to take note and obey their recommendations. These days, it is as much the choice of an unexpected reviewer, or the sheer power or wit or originality of the review, which urges the prospective buyer into the bookshop.

Test 3

PAPER 2 WRITING (1 hour 30 minutes)

Part 1

You **must** answer this question. Write your answer in **180–220** words in an appropriate style.

---

1. You are a member of the college students' committee at an international language college in New Zealand. A TV producer, Kira Linehan, is planning to make a programme about language colleges, including yours. She has asked you for a proposal about what aspects of your college should be included in the programme.

   Read the extract from Ms Linehan's email below. Then, **using the information appropriately**, write a proposal to her, outlining what the programme should include and explaining why, and saying why your ideas would work best.

From: kira@acetv.co.nz
Subject: TV programme

I hope you can help me with this programme. We'd like viewers to get a real feel for what student life is like. But we've only got space to include two or three ideas. We're considering these:

History of your college —————————————————— Interviews
Students ⟵
Different departments
Social life
Accommodation ——————————————— Language class – interesting?

Sports, music, drama, etc

Which of these ideas would work best?

Kira Linehan

Now write your **proposal** to Ms Linehan, as outlined above. You should use your own words as far as possible.

Paper 2 Writing

Part 2

Choose **one** of the following writing tasks. Your answer should follow exactly the instructions given. Write approximately **220–260** words.

---

2   You see the following announcement in a magazine called *Tourism Today*.

> Pop stars, sports personalities and film stars are often the most famous representatives of their countries. Who is the best-known representative of your country? Write an article:
> - telling us about this person
> - explaining why he or she attracts so much interest
> - giving your opinion about the image he or she presents.

Write your **article**.

3   You have been asked to write an information sheet on healthy living for new students from other countries who are attending your college. The information sheet should:
- warn of the possible dangers of an unhealthy lifestyle
- persuade new students that living healthily can be enjoyable
- give advice on how to eat healthily as well as suggestions for how to lead a healthy lifestyle.

Write the **information sheet**.

4   You have been asked to write a report for an international survey about attitudes to jobs in your country. You should:
- describe the ways in which some jobs have gained or lost respect during the past twenty years
- explain why you think this has occurred
- say what other changes in job status may take place in the future.

Write your **report**.

5   Answer **one** of the following two questions based on **one** of the titles below.

(a) Adriana Trigiani: *Big Stone Gap*

A local English language club has asked you to write a review of *Big Stone Gap* for its magazine. The club has male and female members of all ages and your review should comment on which group of club members you feel the story is most likely to appeal to, giving reasons for your opinions.

Write your **review**.

(b) Dick Francis: *In the Frame*

You decide to write an article on *In the Frame* for a cinema website. Your article should comment on why you feel the story would make a good film and should explain whether the English, the Australian or the New Zealand scenes would provide the most interesting part of the film.

Write your **article**.

Test 3

PAPER 3   USE OF ENGLISH (1 hour)

Part 1

For questions **1–12**, read the text below and decide which answer (**A, B, C** or **D**) best fits each gap. There is an example at the beginning (**0**).

Mark your answers **on the separate answer sheet**.

Example:

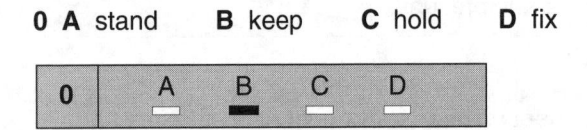

0 A stand   **B** keep   **C** hold   **D** fix

| 0 | A | **B** | C | D |

Holidays in South Carolina

Roaring across the bay in a motorised rubber boat, we were told by the captain to **(0)** ..... our eyes open. With the engine turned off, it wasn't long before half a dozen dolphins came swimming around us. Eventually, two came up **(1)** ..... beside the boat and popped their heads out of the water to give us a wide grin.

Dolphin watching is just one of the many unexpected attractions of a holiday in South Carolina, in the USA. The state has long been popular with golfers and, with dozens of **(2)** ..... in the area, it is **(3)** ..... a golfer's paradise. But even the keenest golfer needs other diversions and we soon found the resorts had plenty to **(4)** ..... .

In fact, Charleston, which is midway along the **(5)** ..... , is one of the most interesting cities in the USA. and is where the first shots in the Civil War were **(6)** ..... . Taking a guided horse and carriage tour through the quiet back streets you get a real **(7)** ..... of the city's past. Strict regulations **(8)** ..... to buildings so that original **(9)** ..... are preserved.

South of Charleston lies Hilton Head, an island resort about 18 km long and **(10)** ..... like a foot. It has a fantastic sandy beach **(11)** ..... the length of the island and this is perfect for all manner of water sports. Alternatively, if you feel like doing nothing, **(12)** ..... a chair and umbrella, head for an open space and just sit back and watch the pelicans diving for fish.

70

1	**A** direct	**B** right	**C** precise	**D** exact
2	**A** courses	**B** pitches	**C** grounds	**D** courts
3	**A** fully	**B** truly	**C** honestly	**D** purely
4	**A** show	**B** provide	**C** offer	**D** supply
5	**A** beach	**B** coast	**C** sea	**D** shore
6	**A** thrown	**B** aimed	**C** pulled	**D** fired
7	**A** significance	**B** meaning	**C** sense	**D** comprehension
8	**A** apply	**B** happen	**C** agree	**D** occur
9	**A** points	**B** characters	**C** factors	**D** features
10	**A** formed	**B** shaped	**C** made	**D** moulded
11	**A** lying	**B** running	**C** going	**D** following
12	**A** charge	**B** lend	**C** hire	**D** loan

Part 2

For questions **13–27**, read the text below and think of the word which best fits each gap. Use only **one** word in each gap. There is an example at the beginning (**0**).

Write your answers **IN CAPITAL LETTERS on the separate answer sheet**.

Example: `0  M O S T`

The Sahara marathon

One of the **(0)** ..... amazing marathon races in the world is the Marathon of the Sands. It takes place every April in the Sahara Desert in the south of Morocco, a part of the world **(13)** ..... temperatures can reach fifty degrees centigrade. The standard length of a marathon is 42.5 kilometres but **(14)** ..... one is 240 kilometres long and takes seven days to complete. It began in 1986 and now attracts about two hundred runners, the majority of **(15)** ..... ages range from seventeen to forty-seven. About half of **(16)** ..... come from France and the rest from all over the world. From Britain it costs £2,500 to enter, **(17)** ..... includes return air fares. The race is rapidly **(18)** ..... more and more popular **(19)** ..... , or perhaps because of, the harsh conditions that runners must endure. They have to carry food and **(20)** ..... else they need **(21)** ..... seven days in a rucksack weighing no more than twelve kilograms. In **(22)** ..... to this, they are given a litre and a half of water every ten kilometres. Incredibly, nearly **(23)** ..... the runners finish the course. **(24)** ..... man, Ibrahim El Joual, took part in every race from 1986 to 2004. Runners do suffer terrible physical hardships. Sometimes they lose toenails and skin peels **(25)** ..... their feet. However, doctors are always on hand to deal **(26)** ..... minor injuries and to make sure that runners do not push **(27)** ..... too far.

Part 3

For questions **28–37**, read the text below. Use the word given in capitals at the end of some of the lines to form a word that fits in the gap **in the same line**. There is an example at the beginning **(0)**.

Write your answers **IN CAPITAL LETTERS** on the separate answer sheet.

Example: `0 A R C H A E O L O G I S T`

Thor Heyerdahl and the *Kon-Tiki* expedition

The Norwegian explorer and **(0)** ..... , Thor Heyerdahl, accomplished	**ARCHAEOLOGY**
many things during his life but his name has become **(28)** ..... linked	**SEPARABLE**
with the *Kon-Tiki* voyage. In 1937, while doing research in the western	
Pacific, Heyerdahl became **(29)** ..... interested in how the Polynesian	**INCREASE**
islands had become populated. He made the observation that ocean	
currents flowed across the Pacific from east to west. Since there were	
cultural **(30)** ..... to be found on either side of this ocean, he was convinced	**SIMILAR**
that South Americans had sailed westwards to populate these islands	
before the eleventh century.	
The **(31)** ..... argument against Heyerdahl's theory was lack of evidence	**CENTRE**
that, at that time, boats existed with the **(32)** ..... to cross such an	**CAPABLE**
(33) ..... of ocean. So a determined Heyerdahl built a primitive raft of	**EXPAND**
balsa wood, named it *Kon-Tiki*, and on April 28th, 1947, left Peru with a	
crew of five. Moved along by the ocean currents, the fragile raft *Kon-Tiki*	
sailed a steady 70 kilometres a day.	
Despite heavy storms, failure never crossed the crew's minds. After 97 days,	
they caught **(34)** ..... of one of the islands. However, due to unusually high	**SEE**
winds they could not land and, realising that a reef presented an **(35)**	**AVOID**
obstacle, they prepared for the inevitable **(36)** ..... . Amazingly, they all	**COLLIDE**
survived the crash, and Heyerdahl had his **(37)**	**PROVE**

Part 4

For questions **38–42**, think of **one** word only which can be used appropriately in all three sentences. Here is an example (**0**).

Example:

0 The committee decided to .... the money equally between the two charities.

I can't believe that John and Maggie have decided to .... up after 20 years of marriage.

To serve a watermelon you need to .... it down the centre with a sharp knife.

Example: | 0 | S | P | L | I | T | | | | | | | | | | |

Write **only** the missing word **IN CAPITAL LETTERS on the separate answer sheet**.

---

38 Although Melissa accepted the invitation, she failed to .... up on the evening of the party.

After three hours of battling against the blizzard, the hikers decided to .... back and head for home.

Whenever she needed help with her maths homework, Chloe would .... to her grandfather, who had taught the subject in his youth.

39 Shall I .... you another cup of tea?

Just look at those black clouds – it's going to .... very soon.

Molly was able to .... out all her troubles to her best friend.

40 Paul is always .... of money by the end of the month.

The boss had to cut .... his holiday in order to sort out the crisis in the factory.

After one of the forwards was sent off, the team were one player .... for the rest of the match.

41 When I call my sister in Australia the .... is so clear I can hardly believe she's on the other side of the world.

Everyone joined in the first .... of the chorus of the song but nobody knew how it went after that.

Do you know what .... of business Charles is in?

42 Eddie is hoping to get a part in the new .... of the musical *Cats*.

They are increasing the .... of ice cream because of greater demand during the hot weather.

Students should note that .... of a current student card entitles them to a 10% discount.

Test 3

Part 5

For questions **43–50**, complete the second sentence so that it has a similar meaning to the first sentence, using the word given. **Do not change the word given**. You must use between **three** and **six** words, including the word given. Here is an example (**0**).

Example:

0 Fernanda refused to wear her sister's old dress.

   NOT

   Fernanda said that .... her sister's old dress.

The gap can be filled with the words 'she would not wear', so you write:

Example: | 0 | SHE WOULD NOT WEAR |

Write the missing words **IN CAPITAL LETTERS on the separate answer sheet**.

---

43 Most of the children ignored what the teacher had told them.

   NOTICE

   Few of the children .... what the teacher had told them.

44 I didn't realise how short the singer was until I saw him onstage.

   MADE

   It was only .... me realise how short the singer was.

45 It's so difficult to create new ideas for the festival every year!

   COME

   How difficult .... with new ideas for the festival every year!

46 The company has a good reputation in the local area.

HIGHLY

The company .... of in the local area.

47 I'm sure Jemma is going to become a famous model one day.

MATTER

I think it's only .... Jemma becomes a famous model.

48 Everyone will enjoy this exhibition because there are no fewer than twenty dinosaurs on display.

MANY

This exhibition will appeal .... as twenty dinosaurs are on display.

49 At the beginning of the programme the panel of experts discussed the media and its importance in education.

DISCUSSION

The panel of experts started the programme .... the media and its importance in education.

50 Barbara's parents were certain that she would be a great tennis player.

DOUBT

Barbara's parents were .... that she would be a great tennis player.

Test 3

PAPER 4 LISTENING (approximately 40 minutes)

Part 1

You will hear three different extracts. For questions **1–6**, choose the answer (**A**, **B** or **C**) which fits best according to what you hear. There are two questions for each extract.

Extract One

You overhear a man telling a friend about a trip to the theatre.

1 The man says that the theatre

    A had recently moved.

    B was overcrowded.

    C was unusually small.

2 The man criticises the actors for

    A lacking enthusiasm.

    B forgetting their lines.

    C wearing inappropriate make-up.

Extract Two

You hear a media interview with a tour operator at a conference on what is called 'responsible' tourism.

3 What distinctive feature of his company is the tour operator keen to stress?

    A It is responsive to local employment needs.

    B It designs tours for selected groups and special interests.

    C It makes limited use of non-renewable sources of energy.

4 He makes the point that the majority of tourists are now

    A conscious of a greater need for social justice.

    B willing to pay additional amounts for responsible tourism.

    C unaware that the choices they make have far-reaching effects.

Paper 4 Listening

Extract Three

You hear two local radio presenters, Laura and Steve, talking about a forthcoming rugby match.

5   What do they agree about?

    A   The ticket allocation has been unfair.

    B   The final result is almost impossible to predict.

    C   The absence of certain players will make for a less exciting game.

6   Listeners who are planning to go to Australia to see the match should

    A   organise their accommodation in advance.

    B   join the official fan club to reduce their travelling costs.

    C   bring their children along to introduce them to the sport.

Test 3

Part 2

You will hear a woman called Kate Assadi talking to a group of people interested in taking up skydiving. For questions **7–14**, complete the sentences.

Skydiving

Kate says that in the USA people from a variety of [**7**] enjoy skydiving.

Kate first tried skydiving when she was a [**8**] and it cost relatively little.

Kate says skydiving can help overcome a fear of [**9**] and increase confidence.

More people are buying skydiving equipment from [**10**] these days.

Kate recently bought a [**11**] at a bargain price.

To become an instructor, a skydiver must have done at least [**12**] previous jumps.

You can find the Parachute Association by contacting the nearest [**13**].

Kate advises people to spend a period of [**14**] learning to skydive.

Part 3

You will hear an interview with an engineer called Roger Moffat, who now works in the film industry. For questions **15–20**, choose the answer (**A**, **B**, **C** or **D**) which fits best according to what you hear.

---

15 How did Roger feel initially about being made redundant?

    A   angry
    B   resigned
    C   depressed
    D   disinterested

16 Roger regards his early days in business as

    A   frustrating.
    B   demanding.
    C   irrelevant.
    D   boring.

17 What does Roger feel is the greatest benefit of running his own business?

    A   He arranges his free time as he pleases.
    B   He gets on better with other people.
    C   He has more leisure time than before.
    D   He is free of an environment he disliked.

18 What is Roger's attitude towards his future?

    A   He considers his position to be no less secure than before.
    B   He thinks he'll be more vulnerable than he used to be.
    C   He'd feel financially more secure working for someone else.
    D   He considers himself too old to change direction again.

19 How can Roger's appraisal of engineers best be summarised?

    A   They are dedicated workers.
    B   They are creative artists.
    C   They are well-balanced realists.
    D   They are powerful leaders.

20 What does Roger find most satisfying about the 'tools of the trade'?

    A   They are intricate beyond belief.
    B   They are the creations of colleagues.
    C   They are theoretical in design.
    D   They are exciting to contemplate.

Part 4

You will hear five short extracts in which people are talking about the importance of eating breakfast.

TASK ONE

For questions **21–25**, choose from the list **A–H** each speaker's occupation.

TASK TWO

For questions **26–30**, choose from the list **A–H** what each speaker says.

While you listen you must complete both tasks.

A stewardess

B swimmer

C researcher

D doctor

E train driver

F journalist

G athlete

H teacher

Speaker 1 [21]
Speaker 2 [22]
Speaker 3 [23]
Speaker 4 [24]
Speaker 5 [25]

A My job makes breakfast impossible.

B My advice is for adults.

C My ideas are original.

D My routine surprises people.

E My planning is worth it.

F My work is respected.

G My advice keeps changing.

H My experience supports a theory.

Speaker 1 [26]
Speaker 2 [27]
Speaker 3 [28]
Speaker 4 [29]
Speaker 5 [30]

PAPER 5 SPEAKING (15 minutes)

There are two examiners. One (the interlocutor) conducts the test, providing you with the necessary materials and explaining what you have to do. The other examiner (the assessor) is introduced to you, but then takes no further part in the interaction.

Part 1 (3 minutes)

The interlocutor first asks you and your partner a few questions. The interlocutor asks candidates for some information about themselves, then widens the scope of the questions by asking about, e.g. candidates' leisure activities, studies, travel and daily life. Candidates are expected to respond to the interlocutor's questions, and listen to what their partner has to say.

Part 2 (a one-minute 'long turn' for each candidate, plus 30-second response from the second candidate)

You are each given the opportunity to talk for about a minute, and to comment briefly after your partner has spoken.

The interlocutor gives you a set of pictures and asks you to talk about them for about one minute. It is important to listen carefully to the interlocutor's instructions. The interlocutor then asks your partner a question about your pictures and your partner responds briefly.

You are then given another set of pictures to look at. Your partner talks about these pictures for about one minute. This time the interlocutor asks you a question about your partner's pictures and you respond briefly.

Part 3 (approximately 4 minutes)

In this part of the test you and your partner are asked to talk together. The interlocutor places a new set of pictures on the table between you. This stimulus provides the basis for a discussion. The interlocutor explains what you have to do.

Part 4 (approximately 4 minutes)

The interlocutor asks some further questions, which leads to a more general discussion of what you have talked about in Part 3. You may comment on your partner's answers if you wish.

Test 4

PAPER 1 READING (1 hour 15 minutes)

Part 1

You are going to read three extracts which are all concerned in some way with music. For questions **1–6**, choose the answer (**A**, **B**, **C** or **D**) which you think fits best according to the text.

Mark your answers **on the separate answer sheet**.

TV Music Programme

The rock music programme *Later...With Jools Holland* occupies a pretty unique position in music television in Britain. Certainly there's no other programme where you can watch a man with a clipboard incompetently interviewing someone on a piano stool, and here the programme has made a successful, if slightly crazy, niche for itself. No teenage pop videos here, no boy bands with carefully marketed brand images or dull-as-dishwater interviews. The programme welcomes the world of rock music with all its mess, its pauses, the unwanted feedback, even the occasional rubbishy nature of some songs.

At times the programme doesn't really seem designed for the viewer's benefit at all. The studio audiences are small, and in some cases rather subdued. The set resembles something from a political discussion programme. It's a set-up that says 'We are musicians; we don't jump through hoops', and this works perfectly. It may not be a sumptuous visual feast, but the programme is likely to be the television engagement that makes a musician feel more like an artist and less like a performing seal.

line 10
line 11
line 12
line 13

The key figure in all this is presenter/performer Jools Holland himself. So uncomfortable does he appear in front of a camera, that it's extremely hard to credit that he has been a television presenter for the best part of 20 years. As far as the programme is concerned, though, Holland's style is ideal.

1 Which words in the second paragraph continue the writer's attack, begun in the first paragraph, on 'teenage pop'?

  A a political discussion programme (line 10)
  B We are musicians (line 10)
  C a sumptuous visual feast (line 11)
  D like a performing seal (lines 12–13)

2 Which possible slogan for the programme best captures the image it projects to the viewer?

  A A music show with endless variety
  B Only the best music
  C Real music with all its imperfections
  D Music that's loud and wild

Opera Audiences

It was curious to say the least, the sheer hostility with which the recent production of *Aïda*, at the Covent Garden Opera House, was received by some audiences. Opera audiences, at the best of times, enjoy a licence to be rude that elsewhere in the theatrical world would be considered bizarre, so the man who shouted 'Rubbish!' was not considered to be behaving in any unseemly fashion. Indeed, he spoke for many.

Patrick Gibson, the director whose work had so irritated the booers, is a grown man who can look after himself, and it is not that I feel in the least outraged on his behalf. But it was not a bad production – indeed, the concession some people have made, that the stage looked beautiful, is to my way of thinking a large one.

What seemed to have annoyed people was an unnatural quality in the acting and movement. Groups moved as on a frieze. Individuals were aware of each other without turning to face each other. Now, I don't necessarily want to see, say, *La Bohème* done this way, but for every opera that calls for naturalism there must be 100 in serious need of something else. A voice behind me was complaining, 'I mean, he's just come back from the war, he hasn't seen her for two years, she hasn't seen him – she doesn't look at him, she doesn't seem pleased . . .' I thought to myself, 'Yes, but they're Ancient Egyptians. Surely they can be allowed to preserve a little of their ancient mystery.'

3   What does the writer say about public reaction to the production?

   A   Even those who were critical admitted that one aspect of it was successful.
   B   It was out of character for an audience at this particular theatre.
   C   He disagreed with public sentiment about the scenery.
   D   He felt personal sympathy towards the director.

4   What point does the writer make about the non-naturalistic approach adopted by the director?

   A   He thinks the approach suits other operas better than it does *Aïda*.
   B   He's not a great fan of the approach but thinks it was appropriate for *Aïda*.
   C   It is ill-informed of critics to single out *Aïda* for adopting this approach.
   D   It would be unfair to blame the approach for the failure of the production.

U2 on tour in the USA

With the roar of applause still filling the night air, the motorcade moves out. There's a howl of sirens, and eight black vehicles leap down a concrete ramp and onto the expressway. We barge through stop signs with our motorcycle escort, waved on by police with scarlet light-sabres. We speed over bridges and plunge through tunnels, the neon glow a smear on the windscreen in the rain. It's completely absurd and really rather thrilling. U2, one of the most famous bands of the last 30 years, are 'doing a runner': Boston's basketball arena to the airport in just over six minutes. Is that a good runner as runners go, I ask?

Band member The Edge replies, 'Indeed it is.' The Edge, or Dave Evans, to give him his real name, wipes the condensation from the window and peers into the blur of blinking lights. He shrugs self-consciously in a manner that suggests the whole thing's preposterous but, at their level, it's the only practical way they can operate.

The same could be said of the gigs themselves. Despite the occasional cry of 'Do some old!', U2 have engineered the impossible feat of still being regarded as contemporary, not bad for a band in their third decade. Rarely in a show are you conscious of being plunged back into the past. Their recent material is so strong you don't even feel the need to go there.

line 20

5   How does The Edge react to the trip to the airport?

   A   excited by all the attention
   B   somewhat embarrassed at their preferential treatment
   C   worried that local people might be inconvenienced
   D   rather irritated to have to leave the concert so abruptly

6   What does 'go there' (line 20) mean?

   A   watch a gig in Boston
   B   voice your approval
   C   go and hear them perform
   D   listen to their old songs

Part 2

You are going to read an extract from a newspaper article. Six paragraphs have been removed from the extract. Choose from the paragraphs **A–G** the one which fits each gap **(7–12)**. There is one extra paragraph which you do not need to use.

Mark your answers **on the separate answer sheet**.

Science Flying in the Face of Gravity

Journalist Tom Mumford joins students using weightlessness to test their theories.

It looked like just another aircraft from the outside. The pilot told his young passengers that it was built in 1964, a Boeing KC-135 refuelling tanker, based on the Boeing 707 passenger craft. But appearances were deceptive, and the 13 students from Europe and America who boarded were in for the flight of their lives. Inside, it had become a long white tunnel.

There were almost no windows, but it was eerily illuminated by lights along the padded walls. Most of the seats had been ripped out, apart from a few at the back, where the pale-faced, budding scientists took their places with the air of condemned men.

| 7 |

Those with the best ideas won a place on this unusual flight, which is best described as the most extraordinary roller-coaster ride yet devised. For the next two hours the Boeing's flight would resemble that of an enormous bird which had lost its reason, shooting upwards towards the heavens before hurtling towards Earth.

| 8 |

In the few silent seconds between ascending and falling, the aircraft and everything inside it become weightless, and the 13 students would, in theory, feel themselves closer to the moon than the Earth. The aircraft took off smoothly enough, but any lingering illusions the young scientists and I had that we were on anything like a scheduled passenger service were quickly dispelled when the pilot put the Boeing into a 45-degree climb which lasted around 20 seconds. The engines strained wildly, blood drained from our heads, and bodies were scattered across the cabin floor.

| 9 |

We floated aimlessly; the idea of going anywhere was itself confusing. Left or right, up or down, no longer had any meaning. Only gravity, by rooting us somewhere, permits us to appreciate the possibility of going somewhere else.

| 10 |

Our first curve completed, there were those who turned green at the thought of the 29 to follow. Thirty curves added up to ten minutes 'space time' for experiments and the Dutch students were soon studying the movements of Leonardo, their robotic cat, hoping to discover how it is that cats always land on their feet.

| 11 |

Next to the slightly stunned acrobatic robocat, a German team from the University of Aachen investigated how the quality of joins in metal is affected by the absence of gravity, with an eye to the construction of tomorrow's space stations.

Another team of students, from Utah State University, examined the possibility of creating solar sails from thin liquid films hardened in ultraviolet sunlight. Their flight was spent attempting to produce the films under microgravity. They believe that once the process is perfected, satellites could be equipped with solar sails that use the sun's radiation just as a yacht's sails use the wind.

| 12 |

This was a feeling that would stay with us for a long time. 'It was an unforgettable experience,' said one of the students. 'I was already aiming to become an astronaut, but now I want to even more.'

A The intention was to achieve a kind of state of grace at the top of each curve. As the pilot cuts the engines at 3,000 metres, the aircraft throws itself still higher by virtue of its own momentum before gravity takes over and it plummets earthwards again.

B After two hours spent swinging between heaven and Earth, that morning's breakfast felt unstable, but the predominant sensation was exhilaration, not nausea.

C After ten seconds of freefall descent, the pilot pulled the aircraft out of its nose dive. The return of gravity was less immediate than its loss, but was still sudden enough to ensure that some of the students came down with a bump.

D At the appropriate moment the device they had built to investigate this was released, floating belly-up, and one of the students succeeded in turning it belly-down with radio-controlled movements. The next curve was nearly its last, however, when another student landed on top of it during a less well-managed return to gravitational pull.

E For 12 months, they had competed with other students from across the continent to participate in the flight. The challenge, offered by the European Space Agency, had been to suggest imaginative experiments to be conducted in weightless conditions.

F It was at that point that the jury of scientists were faced with the task of selecting from these experiments. They were obviously pleased by the quality: 'We need new ideas and new people like this in the space sciences,' a spokesman said.

G Then the engines cut out and the transition to weightlessness was nearly instantaneous. For 20 seconds we conducted a ghostly dance in the unreal silence: the floor had become a vast trampoline, and one footstep was enough to launch us headlong towards the ceiling.

Part 3

You are going to read a newspaper article about a 'mystery visitor' who inspects hotels for a guide book. For questions 13–19, choose the answer (**A, B, C** or **D**) which you think fits best according to the text.

Mark your answers **on the separate answer sheet**.

The Hotel Inspector

Sue Brown judges hotels for a living. Christopher Middleton watched her in action.

One minute into the annual inspection and things are already going wrong for the Globe Hotel. Not that they know it yet. The receptionist reciting room rates over the phone to a potential guest is still blissfully unaware of the identity of the real guest she is doggedly ignoring. 'Hasn't even acknowledged us,' Sue Brown says out of the corner of her mouth. 'Very poor.' It is a classic arrival-phase error, and one that Sue has encountered scores of times in her 11 years as an inspector. 'But this isn't an ordinary three-star place,' she protests. 'It has three *red* stars, and I would expect better.'

To be the possessor of red stars means that the Globe is rated among the top 130 of the 4,000 listed in the hotel guide published by the organisation she works for. However, even before our frosty welcome, a chill has entered the air. Access from the car park has been via an unmanned door, operated by an impersonal buzzer, followed by a long, twisting, deserted corridor leading to the hotel entrance. 'Again, not what I had expected,' says Sue.

Could things get worse? They could. 'We seem to have no record of your booking,' announces the receptionist, in her best sing-song *how-may-I-help-you* voice.

It turns out that a dozen of the hotel's 15 rooms are unoccupied that night. One is on the top floor. It is not to the inspector's taste: stuffiness is one criticism, the other is a gaping panel at the back of the wardrobe, behind which is a large hole in the wall.

When she began her inspecting career, she earned an early reputation for toughness. '*The Woman in Black*, I was known as,' she recalls, 'which was funny, because I never used to wear black. And I've never been too tough.' Not that you would know it the next morning when, after paying her bill, she suddenly reveals her identity to the Globe's general manager, Robin Greaves. From the look on his face, her arrival has caused terror.

Even before she says anything else, he expresses abject apologies for the unpleasant smell in the main lounge. 'We think there's a blocked drain there,' he sighs. 'The whole floor will probably have to come up.' Sue gently suggests that as well as sorting out the plumbing, he might also prevail upon his staff not to usher guests into the room so readily. 'Best, perhaps, to steer them to the other lounge,' she says. Greaves nods with glum enthusiasm and gamely takes notes. He has been at the Globe for only five months, and you can see him struggling to believe Sue when she says that this dissection of the hotel can only be for the good of the place in the long run.

Not that it's all on the negative side. Singled out for commendation are Emma, the assistant manager, and Trudy, the young waitress who dished out a sheaf of notes about the building's 400-year history. Dinner, too, has done enough to maintain the hotel's two-rosette food rating, thereby encouraging Greaves to push his luck a bit. 'So what do we have to do to get three rosettes?' he enquires. Sue's suggestions include: '*Not* serve a pudding that collapses.' The brief flicker of light in Greaves' eyes goes out.

It is Sue Brown's unenviable job to voice the complaints the rest of us more cowardly consumers do not have the courage to articulate. 'Sometimes one can be treading on very delicate ground. I remember, in one case, a woman rang to complain I'd got her son the sack. All I could say was the truth, which was that he'd served me apple pie with his fingers.' Comeback letters involve spurious allegations of everything, from a superior attitude to demanding bribes. 'You come to expect it after a while, but it hurts every time,' she says.

Sue is required not just to relate her findings to the hotelier verbally, but also to send them a full written report. They are, after all, paying for the privilege of her putting them straight. (There is an annual fee for inclusion in the guide.) Nevertheless, being singled out for red-star treatment makes it more than worthwhile. So it is reassuring for Greaves to hear that Sue is not going to recommend that the Globe be stripped of its red stars. That is the good news. The bad is that another inspector will be back in the course of the next two months to make sure that everything has been put right. 'Good,' smiles Greaves unconvincingly. 'We'll look forward to that.'

Paper 1 Reading

13 When Sue Brown arrived at the hotel reception desk,

    A the receptionist pretended not to notice she was there.
    B she was not surprised by what happened there.
    C she decided not to form any judgements immediately.
    D the receptionist was being impolite on the phone.

14 On her arrival at the hotel, Sue was dissatisfied with

    A the temperature in the hotel.
    B the sound of the receptionist's voice.
    C the position of the room she was given.
    D the distance from the car park to the hotel.

15 What does the writer say about Sue's reputation?

    A It has changed.
    B It frightens people.
    C It is thoroughly undeserved.
    D It causes Sue considerable concern.

16 When talking about the problem in the main lounge, Robin Greaves

    A assumes that Sue is unaware of it.
    B blames the problem on other people.
    C doubts that Sue's comments will be of benefit to the hotel.
    D agrees that his lack of experience has contributed to the problem.

17 When Sue makes positive comments about the hotel, Robin Greaves

    A agrees with her views on certain members of his staff.
    B becomes hopeful that she will increase its food rating.
    C finds it impossible to believe that she means them.
    D reminds her that they outweigh her criticisms of it.

18 Angry reactions to Sue's comments on hotels

    A are something she always finds upsetting.
    B sometimes make her regret what she has said.
    C are often caused by the fact that hotels have to pay for them.
    D sometimes indicate that people have not really understood them.

19 When Sue leaves the hotel, Robin Greaves

    A is confident that the next inspection will be better.
    B feels he has succeeded in giving her a good impression.
    C decides to ignore what she has told him about the hotel.
    D tries to look pleased that there will be another inspection.

Test 4

Part 4

You are going to read an article about leadership. For questions **20–34**, choose from the sections (**A–F**). The sections may be chosen more than once.

Mark your answers **on the separate answer sheet**.

In which section of the article are the following mentioned?

deciding to let other people take charge	20
sounding as if you mean what you say	21
not feeling valued in your place of work	22
knowing when it is best not to consult others	23
having the same positive feelings as others	24
considering your professional future	25
wanting to work within certain limits	26
being unaware of your capabilities	27
being prepared to be unpopular	28
realising how leadership may apply to your situation	29
being unfairly blamed	30
being forced to make a big effort	31
being able to turn failure into success	32
achieving more than you set out to do	33
paying attention to other people's opinions	34

CAREER POWER

Get the leading edge – motivate yourself to take full control at work.

A What makes a good leader? A leader is one who inspires, an agent of change, a developer who shows the way forward. Leadership is not about breeding or height – taller being better, as the early theorists believed. It's not simply about intelligence, either. Pat Dixon, author of the book *Making the Difference: Women and Men in the Workplace*, says that leadership is about 'making things happen through people who are as enthusiastic and interested as you are'.

Enthusiasm is a key element and, to convey it and encourage it in others, a good leader should be able to speak out articulately and with conviction. 'It's having the confidence to say "I *believe*" instead of "I think",' maintains Dixon.

B John van Maurik, director of a *Leadership in Management* course, says, 'Most people have a far greater potential for leadership than they realise. The process of becoming a leader is recognising those latent talents, developing them and using them.'

In one sense, we are all born leaders – we just need the right circumstances in which to flourish. While it's quite easy to recognise leadership in the grand sense – be it in the form of figures like Emmeline Pankhurst, Mahatma Gandhi or even Richard Branson – it may be more difficult to relate it to our own workplace. And yet this quality is now regarded as the cornerstone of effective management.

C Consider the best and worst boss you've ever had. They may have been equally good at setting objectives, meeting deadlines and budgets. But what about how they achieved them? The best leader will have motivated you, and may have driven you hard. But he would have also given you support. The worst leader would have made you feel like a small cog in the corporate machinery and kept information from you, and then when things went wrong would have reacted as if it were your fault. The first led (very well); the second simply managed (very badly).

D Leaders and managers can be seen as different animals. Managers tend to enjoy working according to set boundaries. Leaders create their own horizons. 'A good manager can keep even an inefficient company running relatively smoothly,' writes Micheal Shea, the author of *Leadership Rules*. 'But a good leader can transform a demoralised organisation – whether it's a company, a football team or a nation.'

E Whether you're the boss or a middle manager, you can benefit from improving your leadership skills. There are definite lessons to be learnt:

- Leadership is something we do best when we *choose* to do it. So find out where your passions and convictions lie. Next time you feel inspired to lead, harness the energy it gives you and act on it.
- Start *thinking* of yourself as a leader. Your ability to lead is a powerful part of you. Recognise it.
- Collaboration can be fine, but there will be times when firm leadership is required. Experiment with your style. If you are a natural transactor, try being the negotiator. If you always ask for the views of others, try taking the lead. Watch how the outcome is changed by this change in you.
- You have to set goals, then beat them. Look at the demands of your job and define those where being a leader will greatly enhance your effectiveness and career prospects.

F
- Leadership does not simply happen. It can only develop from actually taking the lead, from taking risks and learning from mistakes. Learn how to delegate and motivate; organise and chastise; praise and raise.
- Don't assume that your way of leading will immediately win over colleagues. It may even alienate them. Keep working on your communication skills. *You* don't have to be liked – but your ideas and accomplishments *do*.
- Be visible and accessible to those who are important. But bear in mind that it can lend mystique to maintain a distance.
- You don't have to lead all the time. Be clear on where your contribution is vital and how you can help others to develop as leaders.

Test 4

PAPER 2 WRITING (1 hour 30 minutes)

Part 1

You **must** answer this question. Write your answer in **180–220** words in an appropriate style.

1 While studying at a college in Scotland, you recently joined a book club which allows you to buy books by post. You have had some problems with the service that the book club offers, so you decide to write to customer services.

Read the advertisement for the book club, on which you have made some notes. Then, **using the information appropriately**, write a letter to customer services, saying what is good about the club, explaining what you are dissatisfied with and suggesting improvements to their services.

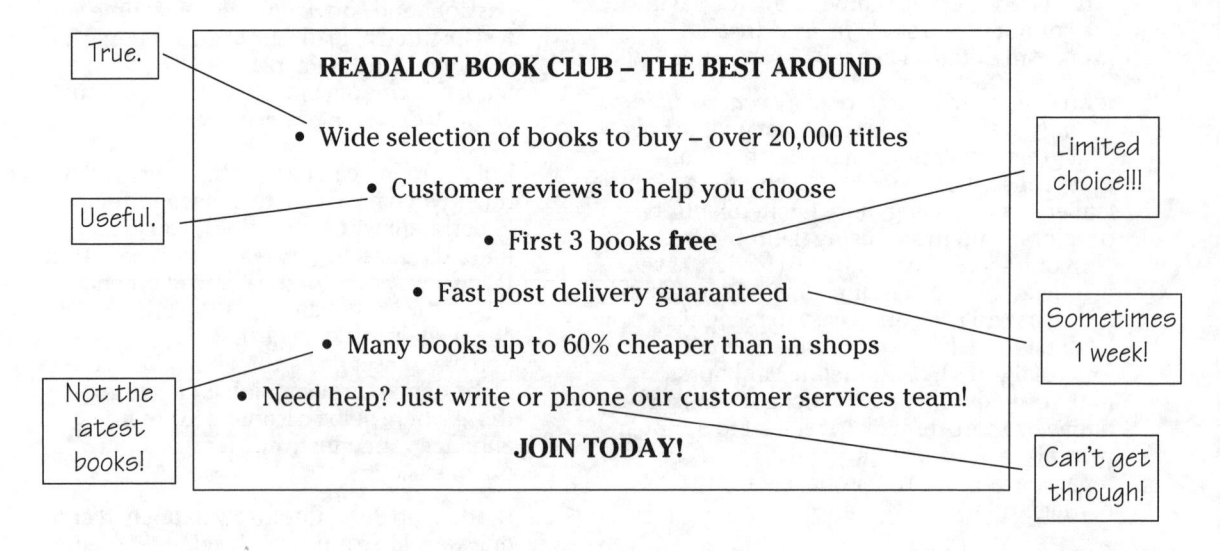

READALOT BOOK CLUB – THE BEST AROUND

- Wide selection of books to buy – over 20,000 titles *[True.]* *[Limited choice!!!]*
- Customer reviews to help you choose *[Useful.]*
- First 3 books **free**
- Fast post delivery guaranteed *[Sometimes 1 week!]*
- Many books up to 60% cheaper than in shops
- Need help? Just write or phone our customer services team! *[Can't get through!]*

[Not the latest books!]

JOIN TODAY!

Now write your **letter** to customer services, as outlined above. You should use your own words as far as possible. You do not need to include the address or the date.

Part 2

Choose **one** of the following writing tasks. Your answer should follow exactly the instructions given. Write approximately **220–260** words.

2   An international magazine has asked its readers to send in a review of **two** different computer games. Write a review for the magazine in which you compare and contrast **two** different computer games, commenting on the following points:
- graphics and visuals
- the appeal of each game
- value for money.

Write your **review**.

3   You see this competition in an international magazine.

> If you were able to travel back to any place and time in history, where and when would you choose? Describe what you might experience and tell us why you would choose this particular place and time. The most interesting entry will be published in the next issue.

Write your **competition entry**.

4   You see the following announcement in an international motoring magazine.

> **HOW TO PASS YOUR DRIVING TEST**
> We would like our readers around the world to share their ideas and experiences.
> Write us an article suggesting how best to prepare for a driving test, and saying what you should or should not do on the day of the test itself.

Write your **article**.

5   Answer **one** of the following two questions based on **one** of the titles below.

(a) Adriana Trigiani: *Big Stone Gap*

Your teacher has asked you to write an essay about *Big Stone Gap*. Your essay should discuss the picture of life in rural Virginia which the story shows and should comment on whether you would like to have been brought up in such a place, giving reasons for your opinions.

Write your **essay**.

(b) Dick Francis: *In the Frame*

Your college would like to organise a monthly Book Club for students who want to practise their English by reading a book and then spending an evening discussing it. Your teacher has asked you to write a report on *In the Frame*. Your report should briefly describe the story and should explain whether you think it would be a suitable choice for the Book Club to read and discuss.

Write your **report**.

Test 4

PAPER 3 USE OF ENGLISH (1 hour)

Part 1

For questions **1–12**, read the text below and decide which answer (**A, B, C** or **D**) best fits each gap. There is an example at the beginning (**0**).

Mark your answers **on the separate answer sheet**.

Example:

0 A kept   **B** remained   **C** lasted   **D** held

| 0 | A | **B** | C | D |

Universal wet weekend

The weather across much of the British Isles **(0)** ..... settled last week, with a good **(1)** ..... of sunshine. On Saturday, the lunchtime temperature at Bridlington in the north-east of England was 28.2 °C, which compared favourably with Alicante in southern Spain at 29 °C. The rest of the world, however, was coping with some extreme conditions. A tropical storm, given the name Helen, hit Hong Kong on Saturday morning, though her presence had been **(2)** ..... in advance. From noon on Friday, the showers and **(3)** ..... of rain became more and more frequent so that by midnight on Sunday, thirty-six hours later, there had been 333 mm of rainfall, not far off the **(4)** ..... for the month of August, at 367 mm. Even on Sunday there was a **(5)** ..... in Helen's tail. The town centre of Shanwei, near Hong Kong, was flooded when 468 mm of rain fell in the sixty hours **(6)** ..... up to midday on Sunday, **(7)** ..... twice the normal August rainfall. On the other **(8)** ..... of the globe, tropical storm Gabrielle moved across the Gulf of Mexico and overnight rain **(9)** ..... the usual rainfall for the **(10)** ..... month. Although most of Europe enjoyed sun, the high temperatures were sufficient to set off some **(11)** ..... showers. On Tuesday morning, a thunderstorm at Lyons in eastern France **(12)** ..... 99 mm of rain in just six hours.

Paper 3 Use of English

1	**A** extent	**B** quantity	**C** proportion	**D** deal
2	**A** waited	**B** found	**C** felt	**D** warned
3	**A** outbursts	**B** outbreaks	**C** outputs	**D** outlets
4	**A** general	**B** standard	**C** medium	**D** average
5	**A** sting	**B** prick	**C** stab	**D** poke
6	**A** going	**B** leading	**C** taking	**D** approaching
7	**A** only	**B** fairly	**C** hardly	**D** nearly
8	**A** section	**B** side	**C** face	**D** part
9	**A** overtook	**B** exceeded	**C** passed	**D** beat
10	**A** total	**B** sole	**C** single	**D** whole
11	**A** huge	**B** weighty	**C** heavy	**D** strong
12	**A** deposited	**B** placed	**C** lay	**D** set

97

Part 2

For questions **13–27**, read the text below and think of the word which best fits each gap. Use only **one** word in each gap. There is an example at the beginning (**0**).

Write your answers **IN CAPITAL LETTERS on the separate answer sheet**.

Example: | 0 | O | F |

Travelling through Norway

The final part **(0)** ..... our journey started at Gudbrandsdalen, said by many to be the most beautiful of all the valleys in Norway. It was a wonderful landscape, the more so **(13)** ..... being dotted with centuries-old wooden farmhouses, scrupulously maintained in their original condition. At Ringebu the view broadened out and the first high peaks and glaciers came **(14)** ..... view. This view continued to dominate the trip as the train passed through the little village of Dovre, at the foot of the mountains, which give this railway **(15)** ..... name – the Dovre Line. The village lies close **(16)** ..... the pretty village of Dombas, where the track divides. We were heading north, travelling through a pass and descending into country **(17)** ..... was now more tundra-like, **(18)** ..... only occasional birch trees and mountain huts. **(19)** ..... time to time we saw **(20)** ..... lone skier, and once we **(21)** ..... across a man fishing through a hole drilled in the ice. That made us think of food and we made **(22)** ..... way to the restaurant car. We continued through the tundra, the snow sometimes broken **(23)** ..... tracks of elk or reindeer. Although we were not lucky **(24)** ..... to see any, we **(25)** ..... see a pair of Arctic hares later on. In no time at **(26)** ..... , we found we **(27)** ..... arrived in Trondheim.

Part 3

For questions **28–37**, read the text below. Use the word given in capitals at the end of some of the lines to form a word that fits in the gap **in the same line**. There is an example at the beginning (**0**).

Write your answers **IN CAPITAL LETTERS on the separate answer sheet**.

Example: | 0 | D | E | V | E | L | O | P | M | E | N | T | | | | |

The history of skateboarding in the USA

The **(0)** ..... of the sport of skateboarding can be traced back to the early 1890s, when children in California first used wooden boards to 'surf' the streets. During the 1950s, the popularity of the sport increased and manufacturers began producing the first factory-made boards. By the 1960s, the sport had gained an **(28)** ..... following, not just in the USA, but **(29)** ..... .

DEVELOP

IMPRESS
WORLD

However, by 1965, concerns about **(30)** ..... resulted in regulations being introduced to ban skateboarding in most public places in the USA. This **(31)** ..... killed the sport there for the next decade. Companies that had been making a fortune selling skateboards suddenly faced huge **(32)** ..... and many went out of business. Over the next eight years a few **(33)** ..... continued practising the sport but, although they tried hard to raise its profile, they were **(34)** ..... in their efforts.

SAFE

EFFECT

LOSE
ENTHUSIASM
SUCCESS

Then in 1973, some technological breakthroughs revolutionised the sport. The invention of new materials meant that manufacturers could **(35)** ..... the boards but at the same time make them lighter and more manoeuvrable. Such **(36)** ..... also made the boards less dangerous and **(37)** ..... from an increasing number of users led to the installation of special skateboarding parks. Despite the various setbacks it has suffered over the years, the sport is now stronger than ever.

STRONG
IMPROVE
PRESS

Part 4

For questions **38–42**, think of **one** word only which can be used appropriately in all three sentences. Here is an example (**0**).

Example:

0 The committee decided to .... the money equally between the two charities.

I can't believe that John and Maggie have decided to .... up after 20 years of marriage.

To serve a watermelon you need to .... it down the centre with a sharp knife.

Example: | 0 | S | P | L | I | T | | | | | | | | | | |

Write **only** the missing word **IN CAPITAL LETTERS on the separate answer sheet**.

---

38 Despite the poor visibility, the pilot .... the plane safely and didn't have to divert to another airport.

Celia's daughter has .... herself a great job working on the set of the latest James Bond movie.

Carlos kicked the football so hard that it went over the hedge and .... in the neighbour's garden.

39 After a .... of bad luck, things began to change for the company.

Marta knew the training programme would be difficult but she decided that it would be worth it in the long ....

Stephan had been working in the office all day and decided that a .... in the fresh air would do him good.

40 The official listened to the whole story, but it was difficult to tell whether he believed it because his .... did not change at all.

'Yours faithfully' is a polite .... which can be used to close a formal letter.

Her technique isn't perfect but she puts great .... into her piano playing.

41 If your injury is very minor, it will be .... by a nurse rather than by a doctor.

This particular coat is made of a fabric which has been .... with a special substance to make it waterproof.

He had a reputation for being a very demanding boss, but personally I found he .... his staff fairly.

42 There was a nasty .... on the table where the coffee cup had been put down.

When Agnes reached the halfway .... she felt unable to continue the race.

The children all stood up as a .... of respect when the head teacher came into the room.

Part 5

For questions **43–50**, complete the second sentence so that it has a similar meaning to the first sentence, using the word given. **Do not change the word given**. You must use between **three** and **six** words, including the word given. Here is an example (**0**).

Example:

0 Fernanda refused to wear her sister's old dress.

NOT

Fernanda said that .... her sister's old dress.

The gap can be filled with the words 'she would not wear', so you write:

Example: | **0** | SHE WOULD NOT WEAR

Write the missing words **IN CAPITAL LETTERS on the separate answer sheet**.

---

43 My grandfather had completely forgotten that he phoned me last night.

RECOLLECTION

My grandfather didn't .... phoning me last night.

44 If Marc hadn't taken up politics, he might have become a famous art historian.

NAME

If Marc hadn't taken up politics, he might have .... himself as an art historian.

45 The company is unable to guarantee an allocated car-parking space to all employees.

COUNT

The company's employees shouldn't .... allocated a car-parking space.

46 Delia said that she would no longer tolerate her colleagues being rude.

PUT

'I'm not willing .... from my colleagues any longer,' said Delia.

47 This holiday is within our price range, provided we don't go to the expensive restaurants in the tourist centre.

AFFORD

We .... as we avoid the expensive restaurants in the tourist centre.

48 It's very unlikely that Martin will win the 100 metres, as he's out of training.

CHANCE

Martin has almost .... the 100 metres, as he's out of training.

49 Nadia's friend arrived just as she was about to leave the restaurant.

POINT

Nadia was just .... the restaurant when her friend arrived.

50 Paul wasn't able to leave the house all day because of the terrible weather.

IMPOSSIBLE

The terrible weather .... Paul to leave the house all day.

Test 4

PAPER 4　LISTENING (approximately 40 minutes)

Part 1

You will hear three different extracts. For questions **1–6**, choose the answer (**A**, **B** or **C**) which fits best according to what you hear. There are two questions for each extract.

Extract One

You hear part of an interview with a broadcaster who is talking about a series of programmes he presented about landscape painting.

1　Why did he decide to include a picture by a politician?

　A　to point out how painting helps people in different ways

　B　to show some interesting points about styles of painting

　C　to stress that amateur art can equal professional painting

2　How does he feel about the process of drawing?

　A　The activity relaxes him.

　B　He is ashamed of the results.

　C　Concentrating on it is exciting.

Extract Two

You hear an amateur pilot called Gina Nesbit talking about doing aerobatics in her small plane.

3　What does Gina find hard about learning new aerobatic movements?

　A　It is difficult to practise without any instructions.

　B　Trying out some of them makes her feel sick at first.

　C　She can get nervous flying the plane unaccompanied.

4　What gives Gina most pleasure when taking part in competitions?

　A　the relief she feels after completing a sequence of actions

　B　the satisfaction of knowing she has performed accurately

　C　the pride she takes in preparing as thoroughly as possible

Paper 4 Listening

Extract Three

You overhear a chef called George talking to a friend about his daily routine.

5   What does George appreciate most about riding a motorbike?

   A   It allows him to avoid the traffic jams on the way to work.

   B   It reminds him of when he was a teenager.

   C   It gives him some time for himself.

6   Which is George's favourite object in his house?

   A   the kitchen table

   B   the shower

   C   the cooker

Test 4

Part 2

You will hear an art teacher called Rosa Weston giving a talk about making mosaics – works of art that are made out of small pieces of glass and stone. For questions **7–14**, complete the sentences.

Making mosaics

Rosa feels that the real experts in mosaics were the [_____] **7**

Rosa says that the greatest changes have occurred in the [_____] **8** of mosaics.

Until recently, modern mosaics were mostly found in [_____] **9** and swimming pools.

Rosa says that the process of making mosaics calls for both [_____] and [_____] **10**

Most students attend what's called a [_____] **11** as part of their course.

Rosa admits that making mosaics can be compared to doing [_____] **12**

Rosa gives the example of ashtrays and [_____] **13** as objects that are now being made using mosaics.

Rosa has even considered putting a mosaic border on [_____] **14**

106

Paper 4 Listening

Part 3

You will hear part of a radio programme in which two people, Sally White and Martin Jones, are discussing the popularity of audio books. For questions **15–20**, choose the answer (**A**, **B**, **C** or **D**) which fits best according to what you hear.

15 Sally feels that the main advantage of audio books is that they

   A encourage children to read more.
   B make more books accessible to children.
   C save parents from having to read to children.
   D are read by experienced actors.

16 What does Martin say about the woman who came into his shop?

   A She no longer worries about long journeys.
   B Her children used to argue about what to listen to.
   C She no longer takes her children to France.
   D Her children don't like staying in hotels.

17 Martin says that in the USA there is a demand for audio books because people there

   A were the first to obtain audio books.
   B have to drive long distances.
   C are used to listening to the spoken word on the radio.
   D feel that they do not have time to read books.

18 Sally says that authors may record their own books on tape if

   A their book has just been published.
   B they want it read a certain way.
   C they have already read extracts from it aloud.
   D there are no suitable actors available.

19 According to Sally, successful abridgements depend on

   A their closeness to the original.
   B the length of the original.
   C the style of the author.
   D the type of story.

20 Martin feels that unabridged versions

   A are better than abridgements.
   B can be too expensive.
   C contain too much detail.
   D are becoming more popular.

107

Test 4

Part 4

You will hear five short extracts in which people are talking about starting a business.

TASK ONE

For questions **21–25**, choose from the list **A–H** the reason each speaker gives for starting a business.

TASK TWO

For questions **26–30**, choose from the list **A–H** the comment each speaker makes about their business.

While you listen you must complete both tasks.

A careers advice

B redundancy

C family relocation

D taking early retirement

E a newly discovered skill

F an idea in an article

G a disagreement at work

H a friend's advice

Speaker 1 — 21
Speaker 2 — 22
Speaker 3 — 23
Speaker 4 — 24
Speaker 5 — 25

A It has made a lot of money.

B It fills a gap in the market.

C It has added variety to life.

D It was difficult to begin with.

E It is lonely and exhausting.

F It provides little social contact.

G It is causing family problems.

H It has meant a lot of travelling.

Speaker 1 — 26
Speaker 2 — 27
Speaker 3 — 28
Speaker 4 — 29
Speaker 5 — 30

PAPER 5 SPEAKING (15 minutes)

There are two examiners. One (the interlocutor) conducts the test, providing you with the necessary materials and explaining what you have to do. The other examiner (the assessor) is introduced to you, but then takes no further part in the interaction.

Part 1 (3 minutes)

The interlocutor first asks you and your partner a few questions. The interlocutor asks candidates for some information about themselves, then widens the scope of the questions by asking about, e.g. candidates' leisure activities, studies, travel and daily life. Candidates are expected to respond to the interlocutor's and listen to what their partner has to say.

Part 2 (a one-minute 'long turn' for each candidate, plus 30-second response from the second candidate)

You are each given the opportunity to talk for about a minute, and to comment briefly after your partner has spoken.

The interlocutor gives you a set of pictures and asks you to talk about them for about one minute. It is important to listen carefully to the interlocutor's instructions. The interlocutor then asks your partner a question about your pictures and your partner responds briefly.

You are then given another set of pictures to look at. Your partner talks about these pictures for about one minute. This time the interlocutor asks you a question about your partner's pictures and you respond briefly.

Part 3 (approximately 4 minutes)

In this part of the test you and your partner are asked to talk together. The interlocutor places a new set of pictures on the table between you. This stimulus provides the basis for a discussion. The interlocutor explains what you have to do.

Part 4 (approximately 4 minutes)

The interlocutor asks some further questions, which leads to a more general discussion of what you have talked about in Part 3. You may comment on your partner's answers if you wish.

Paper 5 frames

Test 1

Note: In the examination, there will be both an assessor and an interlocutor in the room. The visual material for **Test 1** appears on pages C1 and C2 (Part 2), and C3 (Part 3).

Part 1 3 minutes (5 minutes for groups of three)

Interlocutor: Good morning/afternoon/evening. My name is .... and this is my colleague ....

And your names are?

Can I have your mark sheets, please?

Thank you.

First of all, we'd like to know something about you.

Select one or two questions and ask candidates in turn, as appropriate.

- Where are you from?
- What do you do here/there?
- How long have you been studying English?
- What do you enjoy most about learning English?

Select one or more questions from any of the following categories, as appropriate.

Learning

- Do you prefer studying on your own or with other people? .... (Why?)
- How important have teachers been in your life so far?

Places

- What is the most memorable place you have ever visited?
- Which is the most important room in your house? .... (Why is that?)

Health and fitness

- What do you do to keep fit?
- If you had the opportunity to learn a new sport, what would it be? .... (Why?)

Paper 5 frames

Part 2 4 minutes (6 minutes for groups of three)

Groups of people

Pieces of paper

Interlocutor:	In this part of the test, I'm going to give each of you three pictures. I'd like you to talk about them on your own for about a minute, and also to answer a question briefly about your partner's pictures.
	(Candidate A), it's your turn first. Here are your pictures. They show different groups of people.
	Indicate the pictures on page C1 to the candidates.
	I'd like you to compare two of the pictures, and say what responsibilities the members have as a group, and how they might depend on each other.
	All right?
Candidate A:	[*1 minute*]
Interlocutor:	Thank you.
	(Candidate B), which group do you think would be the most interesting to belong to?
Candidate B:	[*Approximately 30 seconds*]
Interlocutor:	Thank you.
	Now, *(Candidate B)*, here are your pictures. They show people with pieces of paper.
	Indicate the pictures on page C2 to the candidates.
	I'd like you to compare two of the pictures, and say what significance the pieces of paper might have, and how the people might be feeling.
	All right?
Candidate B:	[*1 minute*]
Interlocutor:	Thank you.
	(Candidate A), which pieces of paper do you think look the most important?
Candidate A:	[*Approximately 30 seconds*]
Interlocutor:	Thank you.

Paper 5 frames

Parts 3 and 4 8 minutes (12 minutes for groups of three)

What's important?

Part 3

Interlocutor:	Now, I'd like you to talk about something together for about three minutes. *(5 minutes for groups of three)*
	Here are some pictures of things which are important at different stages of people's lives.
	Indicate the pictures on page C3 to the candidates.
	First, talk to each other about how our attitudes towards these things might change at different stages in our lives. Then decide what the greatest priority might be at each of these stages.
	All right?
Candidates:	[*3 minutes (5 minutes for groups of three)*]
Interlocutor:	Thank you.

Part 4

Interlocutor: *Select any of the following questions as appropriate:*

- What other things do you consider to be important in life?
- Some people say that the best time in life is when you're young. What's your opinion?
- As people get to know each other better, do you think they become more, or less, tolerant of one another? .... (Why?)
- In your country, what is the general attitude towards elderly people?
- As people grow older, do you think they spend more time thinking about the past, the present or the future? .... (Why?)

Thank you. That is the end of the test.

Select any of the following prompts as appropriate:
- What do you think?
- Do you agree?
- How about you?

Paper 5 frames

Test 2

Note: In the examination, there will be both an assessor and an interlocutor in the room. The visual material for **Test 2** appears on pages C4 and C5 (Part 2), and C6 (Part 3).

Part 1   3 minutes (5 minutes for groups of three)

Interlocutor: Good morning/afternoon/evening. My name is ……. and this is my colleague ……. .

And your names are?

Can I have your mark sheets, please?

Thank you.

First of all, we'd like to know something about you.

Select one or two questions and ask candidates in turn, as appropriate.

- Where are you from?
- What do you do here/there?
- How long have you been studying English?
- What do you enjoy most about learning English?

Select one or more questions from any of the following categories, as appropriate.

Daily life

- How important is the computer in your daily life?
- Is it easy for you to find time to relax every day? ……. (Why? / Why not?)

Friends

- Do you and your friends share the same interests? ……. (Is this a good thing?)
- Do you think you will still have the same friends in ten years' time?

The future

- What do you think you will be doing in five years' time?
- Are you excited or worried about the future? ……. (Why?)

Paper 5 frames

Part 2 4 minutes (6 minutes for groups of three)

Being accurate

Prized possessions

Interlocutor: In this part of the test, I'm going to give each of you three pictures. I'd like you to talk about them on your own for about a minute, and also to answer a question briefly about your partner's pictures.

(Candidate A), it's your turn first. Here are your pictures. They show different situations in which being accurate is important.

Indicate the pictures on page C4 to the candidates.

I'd like you to compare two of the pictures, and say how important it is for the people to be accurate in these situations, and what might happen if they were not.

All right?

Candidate A: [*1 minute*]

Interlocutor: Thank you.

(Candidate B), in which situation do you think being accurate is the most important?

Candidate B: [*Approximately 30 seconds*]

Interlocutor: Thank you.

Now, *(Candidate B)*, here are your pictures. They show people with possessions they are proud of.

Indicate the pictures on page C5 to the candidates.

I'd like you to compare two of the pictures, and say why the possessions might be important to these people, and how the people might feel if they no longer had them.

All right?

Candidate B: [*1 minute*]

Interlocutor: Thank you.

(Candidate A), which of these people do you think values their possessions the most?

Candidate A: [*Approximately 30 seconds*]

Interlocutor: Thank you.

Paper 5 frames

Parts 3 and 4   8 minutes (12 minutes for groups of three)

Design a T-shirt

Part 3

Interlocutor: Now, I'd like you to talk about something together for about three minutes. *(5 minutes for groups of three)*

I'd like you to imagine that you are helping to design a T-shirt which will be sold to make people more aware of the environment. Here are some designs to consider for the T-shirt.

Indicate the pictures on page C6 to the candidates.

First, talk to each other about how successful these designs might be in raising awareness of the environment. Then decide which design would be the most appropriate for the T-shirt.

All right?

Candidates: [*3 minutes (5 minutes for groups of three)*]

Interlocutor: Thank you.

Part 4

Interlocutor: *Select any of the following questions as appropriate:*

- What other ways are there of making people more aware of the environment?
- Who do you think should be responsible for protecting the environment – the government or we as individuals? .... (Why?)
- Some people say it is too late to reverse the damage we have done to the environment. What's your opinion?
- What role does the countryside have in our lives nowadays?
- People say: 'It's the simple things in life that make it worth living.' How far do you agree with this?

Thank you. That is the end of the test.

> *Select any of the following prompts as appropriate:*
> - What do you think?
> - Do you agree?
> - How about you?

Paper 5 frames

Test 3

Note: In the examination, there will be both an assessor and an interlocutor in the room. The visual material for **Test 3** appears on pages C7 and C8 (Part 2), and C9 (Part 3).

Part 1   3 minutes (5 minutes for groups of three)

Interlocutor: Good morning/afternoon/evening. My name is ……. and this is my colleague ……. .

And your names are?

Can I have your mark sheets, please?

Thank you.

First of all, we'd like to know something about you.

Select one or two questions and ask candidates in turn, as appropriate.

- Where are you from?
- What do you do here/there?
- How long have you been studying English?
- What do you enjoy most about learning English?

Select one or more questions from any of the following categories, as appropriate.

Leisure

- What do you do to relax after a busy day?
- How important is music in your life?

Travel

- Where would you like to go for your next holiday? ……. (Why?)
- What do you enjoy most about being on holiday?

People

- Who has had the greatest influence on your life so far?
- How easy is it for you to meet new people?

Paper 5 frames

Part 2 4 minutes (6 minutes for groups of three)

Flowers

Observing things

Interlocutor:	In this part of the test, I'm going to give each of you three pictures. I'd like you to talk about them on your own for about a minute, and also to answer a question briefly about your partner's pictures.
	(Candidate A), it's your turn first. Here are your pictures. They show people with flowers in different situations.
	Indicate the pictures on page C7 to the candidates.
	I'd like you to compare two of the pictures, and say what significance the flowers might have for the people concerned, and how they might be feeling.
	All right?
Candidate A:	[*1 minute*]
Interlocutor:	Thank you.
	(Candidate B), who do you think has taken the most care choosing their flowers?
Candidate B:	[*Approximately 30 seconds*]
Interlocutor:	Thank you.
	Now, *(Candidate B)*, here are your pictures. They show people observing different things.
	Indicate the pictures on page C8 to the candidates.
	I'd like you to compare two of the pictures, and say what you think the people might be observing, and why.
	All right?
Candidate B:	[*1 minute*]
Interlocutor:	Thank you.
	(Candidate A), who do you think is showing the most interest in what they are observing?
Candidate A:	[*Approximately 30 seconds*]
Interlocutor:	Thank you.

Paper 5 frames

Parts 3 and 4 8 minutes (12 minutes for groups of three)

Understanding between cultures

Part 3

Interlocutor: Now, I'd like you to talk about something together for about three minutes. *(5 minutes for groups of three)*

I'd like you to imagine that an international organisation wants to encourage greater understanding between people of different cultures. Here are some ideas being considered.

Indicate the pictures on page C9 to the candidates.

First, talk to each other about how effective these ideas might be in encouraging understanding between different cultures. Then decide which two would be the most effective.

All right?

Candidates: [*3 minutes (5 minutes for groups of three)*]

Interlocutor: Thank you.

Part 4

Interlocutor: *Select any of the following questions as appropriate:*

- What can people learn by travelling to different countries?
- Some people say that people are the same the world over. What's your view?
- What can people do in their everyday lives to understand each other better?
- How important is it for people to learn different languages .... ? (Why?)
- Do you think that in future our national characteristics will disappear? .... (Why? / Why not?)

Thank you. That is the end of the test.

> *Select any of the following prompts as appropriate:*
>
> - What do you think?
> - Do you agree?
> - How about you?

Paper 5 frames

Test 4

Note: In the examination, there will be both an assessor and an interlocutor in the room. The visual material for **Test 4** appears on pages C10 and C11 (Part 2), and C12 (Part 3).

Part 1 3 minutes (5 minutes for groups of three)

Interlocutor: Good morning/afternoon/evening. My name is .... and this is my colleague ....

And your names are?

Can I have your mark sheets, please?

Thank you.

First of all, we'd like to know something about you.

Select one or two questions and ask candidates in turn, as appropriate.

- Where are you from?
- What do you do here/there?
- How long have you been studying English?
- What do you enjoy most about learning English?

Select one or more questions from any of the following categories, as appropriate.

Personal experience

- In what ways do you hope to use your English in the future?
- Looking back on your life, what has been a memorable event for you?

The media

- Do you prefer watching films at home or in the cinema? .... (Why?)
- How important are newspapers for you? .... (Why do you say that?)

Travel

- What advice would you give to someone coming to visit your country?
- Would you consider going on holiday on your own? .... (Why? / Why not?)

Paper 5 frames

Part 2 4 minutes (6 minutes for groups of three)

Head for heights

Sleepers

Interlocutor: In this part of the test, I'm going to give each of you three pictures. I'd like you to talk about them on your own for about a minute, and also to answer a question briefly about your partner's pictures.

(Candidate A), it's your turn first. Here are your pictures. They show photographs taken from high places.

Indicate the pictures on page C10 to the candidates.

I'd like you to compare two of the pictures, and say how the people might be feeling, and how difficult it might have been to take the photographs.

All right?

Candidate A: [*1 minute*]

Interlocutor: Thank you.

(Candidate B), which photograph do you think best captures the sensation of height?

Candidate B: [*Approximately 30 seconds*]

Interlocutor: Thank you.

Now, *(Candidate B)*, here are your pictures. They show people who are asleep.

Indicate the pictures on page C11 to the candidates.

I'd like you to compare two of the pictures, and say why the people might have fallen asleep, and how they might feel when they wake up.

All right?

Candidate B: [*1 minute*]

Interlocutor: Thank you.

(Candidate A), who do you think will benefit most from their sleep?

Candidate A: [*Approximately 30 seconds*]

Interlocutor: Thank you.

Paper 5 frames

Parts 3 and 4   8 minutes (12 minutes for groups of three)

Famous events

Part 3

Interlocutor: Now, I'd like you to talk about something together for about three minutes. (*5 minutes for groups of three*)

Here are some pictures showing when some famous events first took place.

Indicate the pictures on page C12 to the candidates.

First, talk to each other about the effect each of these events has had on the world we live in. Then decide which one has had the greatest influence on people's lives.

All right?

Candidates: [*3 minutes (5 minutes for groups of three)*]

Interlocutor: Thank you.

Part 4

Interlocutor: *Select any of the following questions as appropriate:*

- Which famous event would you like to have been involved in? .... (Why?)
- How important is it to enjoy new experiences in life? .... (Why?)
- Some people say nothing can be achieved without effort. How far do you agree with this?
- What aspects of life today do you think will be remembered in the future?
- How do you think life will change during this century?

Thank you. That is the end of the test.

> *Select any of the following prompts as appropriate:*
> - What do you think?
> - Do you agree?
> - How about you?

121

Marks and results

Paper 1 Reading

Candidates record their answers in pencil on a separate answer sheet. Two marks are given for each correct answer in **Parts 1, 2** and **3** and one mark is given for each correct answer in **Part 4**. The total score is then weighted to 40 marks for the whole Reading paper.

Paper 2 Writing

General Impression Mark Scheme

A General Impression Mark Scheme is used in conjunction with a Task-specific Mark Scheme, which focuses on criteria specific to each particular task. The General Impression Mark Scheme summarises the content, organisation and cohesion, range of structures and vocabulary, register and format, and target reader indicated in each task.

A summary of the General Impression Mark Scheme is given below. Trained examiners, who are co-ordinated prior to each examination session, work with a more detailed version, which is subject to updating. The CAE General Impression Mark Scheme is interpreted at Council of Europe, Common European Framework Level C1.

* Candidates who do not address all the content points will be penalised for dealing inadequately with the requirements of the task. Candidates who fully satisfy the **Band 3** descriptor are likely to demonstrate an adequate performance at CAE level.

Band 5	For a **Band 5** to be awarded, the candidate's writing has a very positive effect on the target reader. The content is relevant* and the topic is fully developed. Information and ideas are skilfully organised through a range of cohesive devices, which are used to good effect. A wide range of complex structures and vocabulary is used effectively. Errors are minimal, and inaccuracies which do occur have no impact on communication. Register and format are consistently appropriate to the purpose of the task and the audience.
Band 4	For a **Band 4** to be awarded, the candidate's writing has a positive effect on the target reader. The content is relevant* and the topic is developed. Information and ideas are clearly organised through the use of a variety of cohesive devices. A good range of complex structures and vocabulary is used. Some errors may occur with vocabulary and when complex language is attempted, but these do not cause difficulty for the reader. Register and format are usually appropriate to the purpose of the task and the audience.
Band 3	For a **Band 3** to be awarded, the candidate's writing has a satisfactory effect on the target reader. The content is relevant* with some development of the topic. Information and ideas are generally organised logically, though cohesive devices may not always be used appropriately. A satisfactory range of structures and vocabulary is used, though word choice may lack precision. Errors which do occur do not cause difficulty for the reader. Register and format are reasonably appropriate to the purpose of the task and the audience.
Band 2	For a **Band 2** to be awarded, the candidate's writing has a negative effect on the target reader. The content is not always relevant. Information and ideas are inadequately organised and sometimes incoherent, with inaccurate use of cohesive devices. The range of structures and vocabulary is limited and/or repetitive, and errors may be basic or cause difficulty for the reader. Register and format are sometimes inappropriate to the purpose of the task and the audience.
Band 1	For a **Band 1** to be awarded, the candidate's writing has a very negative effect on the target reader. The content is often irrelevant. Information and ideas are poorly organised and often incoherent and there is minimal use of cohesive devices. The range of structures and vocabulary is severely limited, and errors frequently cause considerable difficulty for the reader. Register and format are often inappropriate to the purpose of the task and the audience.
Band 0	For a **Band zero** to be awarded, there is either too little language for assessment or the candidate's writing is totally irrelevant or illegible.

Paper 2 sample answers and examiner's comments

Sample A (Test 1, Question 1 – Report)

> Riverdale College Sports Club is advertised as one of the best clubs of New Zealand. You can't avoid to say it's good, but on the other hand lots of customers are complaining about it.
>
> First of all, there are lots of rooms, but there isn't a place to relax or have a drink after the activities: we ought to add a relax-room in order to create a more familiar atmosphere.
>
> Another big problem is the shower room: showers are always broken so that people have to wait long hours before finding a free one. It makes customers feel unsatisfied, so word rapidly gets around and this creates a bad image of the club.
>
> People is also complaining about the fitness room which is always crowded: we should create another one in order to inable customers to feel better.
>
> We can also add organised classes because people who come here for the first time often don't know what to do.
>
> I also suggest to change the open-days: people who work from Monday to Friday don't have time to come here, so they will probably choose another club.
>
> All in all, I can say that a satisfied customer is the key to success, so we should improve everithing we can paying more attention to the atmosphere and, in particular, to the comfort.

Comments

Content (points covered)
Omission: no mention of persuading Principal to fund changes. Other points addressed and expanded well.

Organisation and cohesion
Reasonable paragraphing but weak introduction and conclusion.

Range
Reasonable range.

Accuracy
Several errors, e.g. 'People is, suggest to change'.

Appropriacy of register and format
Consistently appropriate.

Target reader
Would not be fully informed.

Band 2

Marks and results

Sample B (Test 2, Question 1 – Letter)

> DEAR SIR,
> I would like to express my complaint about the programme "English conversation in a week" recorded on CD's.
>
> I bought these disks to improve my English but I should say that the programme has some shortcomings.
>
> First of all, it does not have business conversations as it is indicated in the advertisement.
>
> Secondly, the time given for listening and repeating is not enough. As for me, I would like to have more time for this activity.
>
> The last point is concerned the cost of the disks. Taking into account that the programme has several weak points, every disk costs twenty euro. I think it would be reasonable to reduce the price and include the material concerning business. I suppose that there are many people who want to speak English for their jobs and in everyday life and who are learning the language by means of your CD's.
>
> I would be very grateful to you if you pay attention to my letter and make changes in your programme for your customers.
>
> But for this very case, I would like to get my money back because the programme does not correspond to what was said in the advertisement.
>
> Best wishes,
> Your client,

Comments

Content
All points covered and expanded.

Organisation and cohesion
Clearly organised and paragraphed.

Range
Reasonable range of structure and vocabulary, but not always appropriate, e.g. 'express my complaint'.

Accuracy
Reasonably accurate but awkward in places.

Appropriacy of register and format
Not always consistent, e.g. 'Best wishes'.

Target reader
Would be informed.

Band 3

Sample C (Test 2, Question 2 – Proposal)

Dear Sir Principal,
I have decided to write this letter to you in order to inform you that I am willing to start a monthly magazine in English for all of the students at this college. The reasons that I have decided to start this magazine are many. First of all I like the idea of being able to inform the unaware students of important facts, social events. I also think that our college's students need more knowledge about what is happening out of college's borders.

The first issue would include some interviews of our teachers concerning our college, some artistic information, or lyrics from the most famous song of the month, a programme of all the exhibitions of this month that will take place in our college and an environmental survey that has actually been done from a school team and is based on information that they collected by some local residents. It would also include a special article from me, explaining the reasons I wanted to start publishing this college magazine.

I hope I have your agreement about starting publishing this magazine because as I think, it is an opportunity for all of the students to purchase information in a more informal and "teenage" way, in contrary with the formal style in which all articles in daily newspapers are written.

In addition, I would like to ask you if you are willing to give us financial support by just paying the fifty percent of the first issue's costs. All the other issues's costs will be payed by the previous's profits and all the extra money will be donated to Unicef in order to help the poor and helpless children all around the world.

I hope I have your full agreement on this subject.

Yours sincerely,

Comments

Content
All points addressed. Task reasonably achieved, with some attempt at expansion.

Organisation and cohesion
Clearly organised and paragraphed. Letter format acceptable, but headings would be better.

Range
Adequate.

Accuracy
Some non-impeding errors, often resulting from ambition, e.g. *the unaware students / out of college's borders / in contrary with*.

Appropriacy of register and format
Consistently appropriate. Problems with opening formula.

Target reader
Would be informed.

Band 3

Marks and results

Sample D (Test 2, Question 5 (a) – Article)

> The two relationships I want to write about are Ave Maria's relationships with her father and her relationship with Jack.
>
> Ave Maria has two fathers. Her real father is Mario, an Italian. Her mother left Italy when she got a baby. She got married with an American man who\s name is Fred and Ave Maria thought Fred was her father. She only learnt the true after her parents both are died and her mother left her a letter. She never feel close to Fred and so she is not surprise that he was not her father. But her feelings about both fathers are very confused.
>
> At the beginning of the book Ave Maria thinks that she will never marry someone. But she and Jack fell in love and they get married. They have a wonderful travel to Italy and spend time with her real father.
>
> In the end I think Ave Maria's relationship with her fathers is more important to her than her relationship with Jack. This is because her relationship with her fathers has more of an effect on her character and make her the person she is. I think this relationship with influence to her relationship with her husband and with her future children. From my pint of view, her relationship with Jack is much more simple as her relationship with her fathers.

Comments

Content
All the points are addressed but not in a very balanced way, as the candidate does not say much about the second relationship.

Organisation and cohesion
The article is in clear paragraphs but it reads more like a class composition than an article.

Range
Although there is some evidence of range in terms of both structure and vocabulary, in places the writing feels a little repetitive. There are, for example, seven uses of the word *relationship* in the final paragraph.

Accuracy
There are a number of errors throughout the piece, especially when more ambitious language is attempted.

Appropriacy of register and format
Consistent.

Target reader
Would have some information about which of Ave Maria's relationships the writer finds interesting.

Band 3

Sample E (Test 3, Question 2 – Article)

> Mexican Proud.
>
> Mexico is a vast country that has given birth to many personalities well known around the world. One of them certainly is Pedro Infante singer and film star of the known "Golden Era of Film making" (in Mexico 1950) who tragically died in an airplane accident.
>
> Pedro Infante could reflect the esence of being mexican cheerful, warmhearted, sincere and of course a good tequila drinker. People that knew him closer say that he was the same on his movies and on his personal life. He had "that something" that grab the attention of the people around him. His songs are strictly for mexican parties where the tequila is drunk in good quantities, and the people enjoy to dance, where being "macho" is the correct thing and carrying a gun is a way of show and get respect. His image of "mexican macho" with his moustache and his hat arriving, to the "cantina" with a bottle of tequila and with the "Mariachi" behind singing colorfull songs in unforgetable!

Comments

Content
All points addressed.

Organisation and cohesion
Clearly organised into paragraphs.

Range
Adequate range of vocabulary and structure.

Accuracy
A number of non-impeding errors, e.g. *he was the same on his movies / the people enjoy to dance / a way of show and get respect / colorfull.*

Appropriacy of register and format
Consistent with article genre with attempt to engage reader.

Target reader
Would be engaged and interested.

Band 3

Marks and results

Sample F (Test 4, Question 3 – Competition entry)

> If I was to be given the opportunity of traveling back in time, I would certainly stop in Britain in the time of the reign of the first female English queen – Elizabeth I. I have always been fascinated by this extraordinary historical figure who had such significant influence on this country and its history.
>
> This decision of my past time destination occurs to me quite naturally for history is one of my life-long interests, especially the period around 15th and 16th century. Although I am aware that living in those times was not as comfortable and easy as it is nowadays, thanks to all the inventions of the modern life, I would love to explore the spirit of the life centuries ago. Living in England in the 16th century might take me to London, where Shakespeare just opened his Globe. Watching one of his famous plays I could catch a glimpse of the queen, dressed in clothes of an ordinary woman, surrounded by her servants. She was said to attend the theatre in disguise in order to amuse herself and escape from the formality of her royal court.
>
> My next destination could be a lively market, where I would watch the hussle of the everyday life of ordinary people comming there to sell handmade potery and fabrics or buy some fresh eggs and bread. My main interest would be the queen, as I mentioned before. Having seen a great documentary based on her life recently I can't help wondering how this subtle woman managed to rule her country succesfully for so many years. She must have been a person of a magnificent character and skills if she was to lead the country in those unsettled times of continuous wars against Spain and France. She defeated rebelion initiated by her cousin Mary and by many others, who didn't like to see her on the throne. Surprisingly, she had never got married. It might have been a part of her strategy how to keep the fragile peace. But it would be her devotion for the nation and her people's wellfare as she once proclaimed. That is why I want to travel to the Elizabethan times and meet this fantastic person whose strength and personal experience could teach me a lot and whom I cannot help to admire.

Comments

Content
All points covered and developed.

Organisation and cohesion
Very well organised, clearly paragraphed, good internal cohesion.

Range
Excellent, with some genuinely sophisticated language, e.g. 'attend the theatre in disguise in order to amuse herself and escape from the formality of her royal court'.

Accuracy
Some minor, non-impeding errors (NB not a flawless performance).

Appropriacy of register and format
Appropriate, with very good, natural tone.

Target reader
Would be interested and informed.

Band 5

Sample G (Test 4, Question 4 – Article)

The best way to pass driving test

Driving test is one of the most dificult tests and needs pleanty of preparation, as well as some skils, so that the way in which people are preparing is very imtortant. In may experiences the best way to lern driving is to attend special cours and trying to drive as much as possible. I drive a lot because my frind allowed me to drive his car when we were driving somewhere. Next thing is to lern principles of driving. I personely bought a book "Drive well" which really help me to go through all signs. God idea is to observe the singns even if you do not drive. It helps to remember them.

Imtortant is to be good at parking and all of that staff. Best way to do that is to do that in special places where is no cars. My advise on the day of the exam is to be relax and do not be nervous. First of all, person taken exam should not be sleepy. So that, I recomend to go to bed early. People who cannot sleep should not take any pils because it is very dangerous andmay lead to an accident. Exam takers should have brekfast on the day of the exam, even if do not do it usually. It really work because then you can fell less nervouse. As I said above taking driving test is not easy but when it is follow by a good preparation it seems to be really easy.

Comments

Content
All points addressed.

Organisation and cohesion
Paragraphed, with some attempt to use cohesive devices. Good balance between ideas and test preparation.

Range
Not ambitious, and marred by inaccuracy.

Accuracy
A number of errors and spelling mistakes, e.g. *imtortant / may experiences / frind / Singns*. Language too elementary for this level.

Appropriacy of register and format
Generally consistent, with some inappropriate informality.

Target reader
Would be partially informed but would require patience.

Band 2

Marks and results

Sample H (Test 4, Question 5 (b) – Report)

> Report for Book Club
>
> In the Frame by Dick Francis
>
> The story
> This is a exciting story about a man who studies the murder of his cousin's wife. He is a very brave man who finds himself in very dangerous situations but in the end he can find the answer. He has to travel to the other end of the world and the reader has the chance to go to Australia and New Zealand. We also learn about the strange worlds of horse-racing and art.
>
> Recommendation
> I think that In the Frame will be a very good book to our club to discuss. It is exciting and our club members would enjoy to read it. When I read it I couldn't stop because I very much wanted to know what will happen. From time to time I was thinking that the hero will not survive. Moreover, it was extremely interesting to read about different places of the world.
>
> In addition, the book is good for learn English because it is a modern book and there is a lot of conversation in it and so we can learn the language of today, not the language of past. I learnt a lot of useful vocabulary and expressions from it.
>
> In, short, I want to recommend it for our Book Club. We could spend a very happy evening to discuss it. I think we can, for example, talk about the hero and his character and his relations with other people in the book

Comments

Contents
All the points are fully covered and suitably expanded. Clear reasons are provided to support the recommendation.

Organisation and cohesion
The essay is well organised in clearly connected paragraphs. Good use is made of headings. Appropriate use is made of connectors.

Range
There is some evidence of range as far as both structure and vocabulary are concerned.

Accuracy
The writing is reasonably accurate although it does not always sound very natural. There are a few careless errors, e.g. *exciting / enjoy to read / for learn*, but the candidate always succeeds in conveying their ideas.

Appropriacy of register and format
Consistent.

Target reader
Would be fully informed about the nature of the book and why the candidate thinks it would be a suitable choice for a Book Club to read.

Band 4

Paper 3   Use of English

One mark is given for each correct answer in **Parts 1, 2** and 3. Two marks are given for each correct answer in **Part 4**. For **Part 5**, candidates are awarded a mark of 2, 1 or 0 for each question according to the accuracy of their response. Correct spelling is required in **Parts 2, 3, 4** and **5**. The total mark is subsequently weighted to 40.

Paper 4   Listening

One mark is given for each correct answer. The total is weighted to give a mark out of 40 for the paper.

For security reasons, several versions of the Listening paper are used at each administration of the examination. Before grading, the performance of the candidates in each of the versions is compared and marks adjusted to compensate for any imbalance in levels of difficulty.

Paper 5   Speaking

Candidates are assessed on their own individual performance and not in relation to each other, according to the following five analytical criteria: grammatical resource, vocabulary resource, discourse management, pronunciation and interactive communication. Assessment is based on performance in the whole test and not in particular parts of the test.

Both examiners assess the candidates. The assessor applies detailed analytical scales, and the interlocutor applies a global achievement scale, which is based on the analytical scales.

Analytical scales

Grammatical resource

This refers to the accurate and appropriate use of a range of both simple and complex forms. Performance is viewed in terms of the overall effectiveness of the language used in spoken interaction.

Vocabulary resource

This refers to the candidate's ability to use a wide range of vocabulary to meet task requirements. At CAE level, the tasks require candidates to speculate and exchange views on unfamiliar topics. Performance is viewed in terms of the overall effectiveness of the language used in spoken interaction.

Discourse management

This refers to the candidate's ability to link utterances together to form coherent speech, without undue hesitation. The utterances should be relevant to the tasks and should be arranged logically to develop the themes or arguments required by the tasks.

Pronunciation

This refers to the candidate's ability to produce intelligible utterances to fulfil the task requirements. This includes stress and intonation as well as individual sounds. Examiners put themselves in the position of the non-ESOL specialist and assess the overall impact of the pronunciation and the degree of effort required to understand the candidate.

Interactive communication

This refers to the candidate's ability to take an active part in the development of the discourse. This requires the ability to participate in the range of interactive situations in the test and to develop discussions on a range of topics by initiating and responding appropriately. This also refers to the deployment of strategies to maintain interaction at an appropriate level throughout the test so that the tasks can be fulfilled.

Global achievement

This refers to the candidate's overall effectiveness in dealing with the tasks in the four separate parts of the CAE Speaking test. The global mark is an independent, impression mark which reflects the assessment of the candidate's performance from the interlocutor's perspective.

Marks

Marks for each of the criteria are awarded out of a nine-point scale. Marks for the Speaking test are subsequently weighted to produce a final mark out of 40.

CAE typical minimum adequate performance

The candidate develops the interaction with contributions which are mostly coherent and extended when dealing with the CAE level tasks. Grammar is mostly accurate and vocabulary appropriate. Utterances are understood with very little strain on the listener.

Test 1 Key

Paper 1   Reading (1 hour 15 minutes)

Part 1

1 A   2 C   3 D   4 B   5 A   6 C

Part 2

7 G   8 A   9 B   10 D   11 E   12 C

Part 3

13 C   14 A   15 B   16 D   17 A   18 C   19 B

Part 4

20 E   21 D   22 B   23 A   24 C   25 E   26 D   27 D   28 A   29 C
30 E   31 B   32 A   33 B   34 C

Paper 2   Writing (1 hour 30 minutes)

Task-specific Mark Schemes

Part 1

Question 1

Content (points covered)
For Band 3 or above, the candidate's **report** must:
- make suggestions for improvements/changes
- justify these changes
- persuade the Principal to contribute.

Organisation and cohesion
Clearly organised, possibly with headings.

Range
Language for describing, recommending/suggesting and justifying.

Appropriacy of register and format
Formal to unmarked. Must be consistent.

Target reader
Would be informed.

Part 2

Question 2

Content (points covered)
For Band 3 or above, the candidate's **article** must:
- outline the impact of new technology on their lives
- comment on future changes

Test 1 Key

- explain how these changes may affect them.

Organisation and cohesion
Clearly organised into paragraphs. Early mention of topic(s).

Range
Vocabulary relating to technology, language of explanation and speculation.

Appropriacy of register and format
Appropriately unmarked, informal or formal.

Target reader
Would be informed about the impact of technology on the candidate's life.

Question 3

Content (points covered)
For Band 3 or above, the candidate's **competition entry** must:
- explain why they agree or disagree with the statement
- refer to work, contact with native speakers and travel.

Organisation and cohesion
Clearly organised into paragraphs.

Range
Language of explanation and description, vocabulary relating to language learning.

Appropriacy of register and format
Consistently unmarked, informal or formal.

Target reader
Would have a clear understanding of candidate's point of view and would consider the entry.

Question 4

Content (points covered)
For Band 3 or above, the candidate's **essay** must:
- give opinion on positive and/or negative influence of sponsorship in sport.

Organisation and cohesion
Clearly organised into paragraphs.

Range
Language of describing, explaining and commenting.

Appropriacy of register and format
Formal to unmarked. Must be consistent.

Target reader
Would be informed.

Question 5 (a)

Content (points covered)
For Band 3 or above, the candidate's **report** must:
- describe the two most amusing scenes
- explain why.

Organisation and cohesion
Clearly organised into paragraphs with appropriate linking devices.
Headings may be an advantage.

Test 1 Key

Range
Language of description, opinion and explanation.
Vocabulary related to description of humour and comment on a story.

Appropriacy of register and format
May mix registers if appropriate to approach taken by candidate.

Target reader
Would be informed.

Question 5 (b)

Content (points covered)
For Band 3 or above, the candidate's **review** must:
- describe Charles Todd
- explain why the story would or would not appeal to students at the candidate's college
- give reasons why.

Organisation and cohesion
Clearly organised into paragraphs with appropriate linking devices.

Range
Language of description, opinion and explanation.
Vocabulary related to description of character and comment on a story.

Appropriacy of register and format
May mix registers if appropriate to approach taken by candidate.

Target reader
Would be informed.

Paper 3   Use of English (1 hour)

Part 1

1 C   2 C   3 D   4 A   5 A   6 B   7 A   8 D   9 A   10 B   11 D
12 C

Part 2

13 so   14 an   15 can   16 one   17 any   18 in   19 last / previous / past
20 when   21 but   22 This   23 which   24 as   25 ago / before   26 like
27 and

Part 3

28 pleasure   29 disadvantages   30 preferably   31 pursuit   32 Fortunately
33 deficiency/ies   34 requirement   35 reasonable   36 hazardous   37 uninterrupted

Part 4

38 hit   39 low   40 power   41 touched   42 place

Part 5

43 in danger | of being/getting dismissed/sacked/fired   44 paying attention to | what he/she was
45 lack of experience / inexperience | affect his   46 forget to | keep/stay in touch   47 go/be going
ahead | (exactly) according   48 up (all/any) hope | of finding/getting (himself)   49 sure/certain
how | I would/I'd have/'ve reacted   50 I will/'ll/would/'d be | surprised if

135

Test 1 Key

Paper 4 Listening (approximately 40 minutes)

Part 1
1 A   2 B   3 C   4 A   5 B   6 A

Part 2
7 freedom, achievement (in either order)   8 adventure sports   9 mental preparation
10 ice (fall)   11 perfume   12 toothbrush   13 satisfaction   14 Aiming High

Part 3
15 C   16 C   17 D   18 D   19 A   20 C

Part 4
21 B   22 A   23 C   24 D   25 G   26 A   27 H   28 B   29 C   30 E

Transcript This is the Cambridge Certificate in Advanced English Listening Test. Test One.

I'm going to give you the instructions for this test. I'll introduce each part of the test and give you time to look at the questions.

At the start of each piece you'll hear this sound:

tone

You'll hear each piece twice.

Remember, while you're listening, write your answers on the **question paper**. You'll have five minutes at the end of the test to **copy your answers onto the separate answer sheet**.

There'll now be a pause. Please ask any questions now, because you must not speak during the test.

[pause]

PART 1 Now open your question paper and look at Part One.

[pause]

You'll hear three different extracts. For questions one to six, choose the answer (A, B or C) which fits best according to what you hear. There are two questions for each extract.

Extract 1 You overhear two friends, Gordon and Annabelle, discussing a film called 'A Secret Place', which they have both seen recently. Now look at questions one and two.

[pause]

tone

Gordon: Annabelle, you saw *A Secret Place* the other day, didn't you?

Annabelle:	I did. Interesting, but the action's very patchy – it falls apart here and there.
Gordon:	There isn't a thread you can follow all the way through, is there? I can see what the director . . .
Annabelle:	Yoshiki Muto.
Gordon:	Yeah. I can see what he's trying to do – it's a complex layering of detail, but it just doesn't come off.
Annabelle:	Well, it's a brave attempt. It works for me. Although I have to say, I still really prefer the original novel with its very delicate touch.
Gordon:	I think, though, the film version taps into our emotions more. But what about the ending?
Annabelle:	I'd have enjoyed it more if it hadn't been for that powerful, pounding rock music, which was obviously supposed to emphasise what was happening on screen. But I did like the way I was on the verge of laughing, then almost crying, for that final two or three minutes. Very well done.
Gordon:	Not that it really appeared to sort anything out for our hero.
Annabelle:	Presumably he'll turn up in a sequel soon, with the same old dilemma!
Gordon:	Look forward to that then!

[pause]

tone

Now you'll hear the recording again.

[The recording is repeated.]

[pause]

Extract 2   *You hear part of a radio interview with an architect called Alan Fasman. Now look at questions three and four.*

[pause]

tone

Interviewer:	So, Alan, what's the best way to get good public architecture?
Alan:	Well, people don't want to be challenged by architecture, that's understandable in a way; I'm not one for saying necessarily that public buildings are an appropriate area where people should have a vote to say that this building should go ahead or not. Many of our greatest and most glorious buildings wouldn't exist if that happened. Take St Paul's Cathedral in London – at the time, people were very antagonistic and hated its horrid foreign style. Now everyone adores it; it's a landmark, a sort of emblem of the city, that wouldn't have existed if public opinion had had its way.
Interviewer:	Do other countries do better than us – either in terms of imagination, or in terms of the kind of decision-making we've been talking about?
Alan:	Yes they do – in recent history anyway. The Netherlands is a prime example. A number of the world's leading architects happen to come from there, but the important thing is that the people are very knowledgeable; they learn about architecture in school. They do have a good record for town-planning as well, but that's hardly the point.

Test 1 Key

[pause]

tone

Now you'll hear the recording again.

[The recording is repeated.]

[pause]

Extract 3   *You hear part of a radio interview with the ecologist Lorna Hindle about climate change. Now look at questions five and six.*

[pause]

tone

Interviewer: Why did you decide to publicise climate change in this way?
Lorna: Well, I was really upset about some countries' failure to sign up to pollution agreements; it felt like the science wasn't getting through to the politicians, so I decided to look into what I personally could do. That led me to dream up a cartoon character called Mr Carbon – we all know somebody like him – he's climate-ignorant and makes no effort to save energy. Factories are the obvious villains, of course, but I couldn't do much about them.
Interviewer: So *are* we going to see him in scenes like we get in disaster movies?
Lorna: That's pretty unlikely – you need a lot of alarmist nonsense to make a box office success. But the reality certainly gives cause for concern.
Interviewer: So you came up with the idea of another cartoon character, Mrs Green.
Lorna: Yes – now she pays attention to little things, uses low-energy light bulbs, doesn't leave the TV on standby, goes in for recycling. And, can you believe it, as well as making a huge difference to her climate impact, she'll save one hundred and fifty thousand dollars over her lifetime.
Interviewer: That's incredible!

[pause]

tone

Now you'll hear the recording again.

[The recording is repeated.]

[pause]

*That's the end of Part One.
Now turn to Part Two.*

[pause]

PART 2   *You'll hear a mountaineer called Stella Prime talking about her experience of climbing Mount Everest in the Himalayas. For questions 7 to 14, complete the sentences.*

You now have forty-five seconds to look at Part Two.

[pause]

138

Test 1 Key

tone

Hello. I'm Stella Prime and I'm a mountaineer. I'm here to tell you about climbing Mount Everest in the Himalayas – the world's highest mountain.

I was first bitten by the climbing bug when, as a journalist, I accompanied an expedition on the northeast ridge of Everest some years back. I wanted to write about what made mountaineers tick, and over the couple of months I spent with the expedition, I began to understand the sense of freedom and achievement that mountaineering brings, and I did lots of personal learning and exploration too. I think they were the happiest two months of my life.

Over the next three and a half years, I honed my newly acquired climbing skills on various mountains all over the world. People say: 'Weren't your family surprised by this new interest?' Well, they weren't, because I'd already done numerous similar activities of the sort people like to call 'adventure sports', you know, hang-gliding, scuba diving and so on.

Anyway, eventually I gave up my job, let out my flat and joined the British Everest Expedition. To prepare physically for this, I trained at my local gym – that was the easy part – the bit I found trickier was the mental preparation and I'd learnt that, whilst you have to be physically fit, that is really only half the story.

And there were lots of things that frightened me about Everest. One of them was the icefall that you have to climb through. A friend asked if there was any way I could prepare myself for it. I thought: 'What can I do – put myself in a fridge and look at lumps of ice?'

Everest is certainly not a place for cowards, and it's also certainly not a place for life's luxuries. You don't carry anything that isn't necessary because weight multiplies at high altitudes. The first time I went, as a journalist, I carried my perfume all the way, but it wasn't necessary. You can forget baths and showers on a mountain as well. On my second trip, I didn't even take my toothbrush above seven thousand metres. The only source of water is melted snow. To melt snow you need fuel and fuel is heavy, so you don't melt snow unless you're going to drink it.

The question I'm asked most often is: 'How did you feel when you reached the summit?' Well, I still get emotional when I think about it. Neither of the two climbers with me had been to the top before either. It was tremendously exciting obviously, but I think the overriding thing we all felt was a great sense of satisfaction. That is the thing that stays with me when I look back.

Since then, I've gone on to climb a number of other summits and I plan to tackle Mount Fuji later this year. And of course I've got my new career in TV – as a presenter on the programme *Tomorrow's World*. I'm in demand on the lecturing circuit and my book about my ascent of Everest – *Aiming High* – is a best-seller. So, that's my story. Now, does anyone have any questions?

[pause]

tone

Now you'll hear the recording again.

Test 1 Key

[The recording is repeated.]

[pause]

That's the end of Part Two.
Now turn to Part Three.

[pause]

PART 3   You'll hear part of an interview with a man called Tony Elliott who founded a magazine called 'Time Out'. For questions 15 to 20, choose the answer (A, B, C or D) which fits best according to what you hear. You now have one minute to look at Part Three.

[pause]

tone

Interviewer: . . . OK, welcome back to the programme. Well, for the hundred thousand or more people in London who buy every issue, *Time Out* is an invaluable guide to what's going on in the city. In its lists they can find everything from films, plays, concerts and nightclubs to exhibitions, sports, opera, dance and special events. And I'm talking now to Tony Elliott, the man who started it all, back in 1968. Tony, what gave you the idea?

Tony: Well, back then it was very hard to find out about those things. There were magazines; there was a magazine called *What's On*, which was a weekly, which is still around – rather, kind of, conventional in its approach, and you could look in the evening paper or you could look in the music press, um, to get information, but nothing covered everything all in one place. So I perceived there was a gap and I suppose to some extent I just produced a magazine for myself, and it turned out a lot of other people wanted the same thing.

Interviewer: At first, the magazine was just a sheet sold hand to hand in the street, wasn't it?

Tony: Well, I started with a few like-minded people and we did actually put it into newsagents – people do seem to think we started as a bunch of idealistic amateurs, but I have to say that I think we were actually pretty professional from day one. It was coming out every three weeks so I'd spend three or four days actually going round something like three hundred newsagents. The selling in the street was partly to do with getting copies sold so that we actually had some cash, but it also had this kind of in-built market research thing where you'd show people what you were doing and they'd go, 'Oh really' – and a lot of people said, 'Oh, that's a modern *What's On*; that's what we've been looking for.'

Interviewer: So, did you have any publishing experience before this?

Tony: Mmm, I did a regular column for a magazine at university which was quite serious. It used to do single themes per issue, like provincial theatre or education or racialism, and then when I took it over I promptly changed it into being a kind of contemporary arts magazine. We did interviews with artists, rock stars, writers, people like that.

Interviewer:	Were you still at university when you started *Time Out*?
Tony:	Yeah, technically I was actually on holiday for the summer vacation, and as far as the university was concerned, I was supposed to be going to France to teach. I think I'd told them I would do, because, you know, you go away for a term or a year if you're studying French, and um, then I started doing the magazine.
Interviewer:	And, er, didn't go back.
Tony:	Yes, well, there was a point when I suddenly realised that I was doing what I wanted to do.
Interviewer:	So it soon took off, didn't it? I mean, it was monthly first and then it went weekly, didn't it, in a very short time?
Tony:	Well, it started monthly and then we went three-weekly – for some reason that was the highest frequency we could do. Then we went fortnightly, which is quite a valid frequency for publication, and then inevitably we went weekly – stimulated, I have to say, by the threat of some competition from some people who were starting a similar publication.
Interviewer:	Oh, yes, I was going to say, someone else must have spotted the gap. I mean you identified it, but there must have been big publishing houses who thought, 'Hang on, we can have some of this too.'
Tony:	I think the truth is nobody really realised what the significance of the magazine was, 'cos in a sense it started very tiny, very small, and then built up and built up and a lot of publishers and a lot of advertisers also were very, um, dismissive of our readers. I mean, still, even today, you get occasional accusations like, 'It's not a particularly significant readership' and 'A lot of students read it, don't they?' . . . things like that. People just didn't realise that, um, that we were creating a readership that was very significant.
Interviewer:	The readership's grown up with you as well, hasn't it? A lot of people, I imagine, who were buying it as students in the sixties are now buying it as parents of teenage children these days.
Tony:	That would imply our readership's now older, which isn't the case. And although the numbers have expanded, well it's true that there are more people over thirty-five buying it than there were when it started. The readership hasn't really changed; it's still basically intelligent young people who do things.
Interviewer:	OK, well, we'll take a quick break now and then I'll be back to talk to Tony some more . . .

[pause]

tone

Now you'll hear the recording again.

[The recording is repeated.]

[pause]

That's the end of Part Three.
Now turn to Part Four.

[pause]

Test 1 Key

PART 4 *Part Four consists of two tasks. You'll hear five short extracts in which people are talking about things that have recently happened to them at work. Look at Task One. For questions 21 to 25, choose from the list A to H what each speaker is talking about. Now look at Task Two. For questions 26 to 30, choose from the list A to H the feeling each speaker is expressing. While you listen you must complete both tasks. You now have forty-five seconds to look at Part Four.*

[pause]

tone

Speaker One: So the Head of Department called me in and launched into this long speech about how my messing up the arrangements for his meeting had created all sorts of trouble for him. While he was going on about it, I glanced at the bit of paper in front of him and I saw the signature and I realised it hadn't been me. I knew it wasn't like me anyway. I mean, I get things wrong but only trivial things. It's going to be hilarious when he realises what a fool he's made of himself. I doubt I'll be able to keep a straight face.

[pause]

Speaker Two: Yeah, I was busy and the Area Manager turned up. Well, I wasn't exactly thrilled to see him; it's hardly ever good news. Anyway, he wanted me to start on some other project. I'd been warned that was coming so I didn't have much trouble coming up with reasons for turning it down. He said I'd regret it later but I said I didn't think so, and he left it at that. The thing is, after all these years with the firm, all I get asked to do are the things no one else fancies. It's really got me down – I joined with such high hopes and now I'm so disheartened, it's such a shame.

[pause]

Speaker Three: The ridiculous thing is, I'd always known she couldn't be trusted, but it's in my nature, I guess, to speak my mind. Still, I shouldn't have confided in her what I really thought of the job. It's just that when she asked me, it caught me unawares. It's got me into a lot of trouble now, because of course she's spread it round everyone else. I should just laugh it off, but that's easier said than done. She'd better not come near me for a while, the way I feel I'd give her a piece of my mind. It infuriates me when people do that kind of thing.

[pause]

Speaker Four: Jack came to my office today – we used to get on really well till they moved him upstairs and I hardly see him now – and he said, 'Hey, there's an opening in our office now. I've fixed it so you can have it.' Well, I didn't know what to say – it came right out of the blue. I mean, he's always done me favours and been kind to me but I can't think of anything worse than working there. So I feel awful about letting him down after all he's done for me, but I'm going to turn it down because it's my career, isn't it?

[pause]

Speaker Five: Well, I tried to be my usual tactful self but he took offence. 'So you can't bear to come on this trip with me?' he asked and I said, 'It's not that, it's just that I've been to so many conferences lately, I want a break from them.' And he said, 'But this is the most important of the lot – don't be so stupid.' If I'd reacted to that, we'd have had an enormous row, so I didn't bother. That's the sort of thing that tends to happen with him. He's either all over you or he can't stand you. That's just the way it is – I won't let it bother me, what would be the point? There's nothing I can do about it.

[pause]

tone

Now you'll hear the recording again.

[The recording is repeated.]

[pause]

That's the end of Part Four.

*There'll now be a pause of **five minutes** for you to **copy your answers onto the separate answer sheet**. Be sure to follow the numbering of all the questions. I'll remind you when there's one minute left, so that you're sure to finish in time.*

[Teacher, pause the recording here for five minutes. Remind your students when they have one minute left.]

That's the end of the test. Please stop now. Your supervisor will now collect all the question papers and answer sheets.

Test 2 Key

Paper 1 Reading (1 hour 15 minutes)

Part 1
1 A   2 C   3 A   4 D   5 D   6 A

Part 2
7 D   8 A   9 G   10 E   11 B   12 C

Part 3
13 C   14 A   15 C   16 B   17 C   18 A   19 D

Part 4
20 C   21 B   22 A   23 C   24 B   25 C   26 D   27 A   28 D   29 B
30 C   31 A   32 D   33 C   34 A

Paper 2 Writing (1 hour 30 minutes)

Task-specific Mark Schemes

Part 1

Question 1

Content (points covered)
For Band 3 or above, the candidate's **letter** must:
- explain why bought CDs.
- explain why dissatisfied
- say what the company should do.

Organisation and cohesion
Clearly organised with appropriate opening and closing formulae.

Range
Language of explanation and persuasion.

Appropriacy of register and format
Formal to unmarked. Must be consistent.

Target reader
Would be informed.

Part 2

Question 2

Content (points covered)
For Band 3 or above, the candidate's **proposal** must:
- give a reason for starting the magazine
- suggest some contents for first issue
- state what support and/or financial help is needed.

Organisation and cohesion
Clearly organised into sections/paragraphs. Letter/memo format acceptable.

Range
Vocabulary relating to magazines/writing.
Language of persuasion, explanation and justification.

Appropriacy of register and format
Consistently unmarked or formal.

Target reader
Would be informed about the reasons why a magazine was needed and consider supporting the idea.

Question 3

Content (points covered)
For Band 3 or above, the candidate's **competition entry** must describe the benefits of:
- travelling alone
- travelling with friends
- travelling with family.

Organisation and cohesion
Clearly organised into paragraphs.

Range
Vocabulary relating to travel. Language of evaluation and assessment.

Appropriacy of register and format
Any, as long as consistent.

Target reader
Would consider the entry.

Question 4

Content (points covered)
For Band 3 or above, the candidate's **report** must refer to:
- measures being taken
- their success
- what more could be done with reference to their region.

Organisation and cohesion
Clearly organised into paragraphs. Use of headings desirable.

Range
Vocabulary relating to energy and natural resources. Language of evaluation and recommendation.

Appropriacy of register and format
Consistently formal or unmarked.

Target reader
Would be informed of the measures in place and future requirements.

Question 5 (a)

Content (points covered)
For Band 3 or above, the candidate's **article** must:
- comment on why the relationships between Ave Maria and two other characters of the candidate's choice are interesting
- discuss which of these two relationships is more important to Ave Maria.

Organisation and cohesion
Clearly organised into paragraphs with appropriate linking devices.

Test 2 Key

Range
Language of description, opinion and explanation.
Vocabulary related to description of character and relationships and comment on a story.

Appropriacy of register and format
May mix registers if appropriate to approach taken by candidate.

Target reader
Would be informed.

Question 5 (b)

Content (points covered)
For Band 3 or above, the candidate's **essay** must:
- briefly describe both the beginning and the ending of the story
- explain how effective the candidate feels both these parts of the story are.

Organisation and cohesion
Clearly organised into paragraphs with appropriate linking devices.

Range
Language of description, opinion and explanation.
Vocabulary related to description of plot and comment on a story.

Appropriacy of register and format
Formal to unmarked. Must be consistent.

Target reader
Would be informed.

Paper 3 Use of English (1 hour)

Part 1

1 C   2 B   3 B   4 D   5 B   6 B   7 C   8 C   9 A   10 D   11 C
12 A

Part 2

13 same   14 been   15 an   16 in   17 This/That/It   18 would/must   19 so
20 or   21 there   22 rather/sooner   23 of   24 since   25 from   26 before
27 little

Part 3

28 participants   29 expertise   30 unskilled   31 explanations   32 surprisingly
33 celebrity   34 contributor   35 disastrous   36 painfully   37 considerably

Part 4

38 free   39 claimed   40 badly   41 nature   42 gained

Part 5

43 no intention/thought | of giving   44 made up | his mind OR made his | mind up
45 to | put in   46 be prevented | in   47 see the point | in/of learning OR see any point | in learning
48 circumstances (whatsoever/at all) should | you have/keep/learn   49 pay on time | will result in
50 made a fast/quick/speedy/rapid | recovery

Paper 4 Listening (approximately 40 minutes)

Part 1

1 C   2 B   3 A   4 B   5 C   6 B

Part 2

7 seals   8 wolf   9 oasis   10 root(s)   11 seeds   12 tunnels   13 (polar) bear
14 (the) batteries

Part 3

15 A   16 D   17 D   18 B   19 A   20 C

Part 4

21 G   22 A   23 E   24 D   25 C   26 D   27 A   28 C   29 F   30 H

Transcript

This is the Cambridge Certificate in Advanced English Listening Test. Test Two.

I'm going to give you the instructions for this test. I'll introduce each part of the test and give you time to look at the questions.

At the start of each piece you'll hear this sound:

tone

You'll hear each piece twice.

Remember, while you're listening, write your answers on the **question paper**. You'll have five minutes at the end of the test to **copy your answers onto the separate answer sheet**.

There'll now be a pause. Please ask any questions now, because you must not speak during the test.

[pause]

PART 1

Now open your question paper and look at Part One.

[pause]

You'll hear three different extracts. For questions one to six, choose the answer (A, B or C) which fits best according to what you hear. There are two questions for each extract.

Extract 1

You overhear part of a conversation between the secretary of a golf club and a visitor to the club. Now look at questions one and two.

[pause]

tone

Test 2 Key

Female: Sorry to be late. This club's a bit off the beaten track, isn't it? Thought I'd never find it!
Secretary: You don't have an in-car satellite navigation system, then?
Female: A sat-nav? No I don't, though I suppose I should invest in one. I often have this sort of trouble – getting to a town's a piece of cake, but after that . . . well. It's not so much the cost – my friends all have them and tell me the price is going down all the time. But electronic gadgets aren't my favourite things. Fine when they work; nightmare when they don't. A little black box could hardly have been less useful than my map today, though!
Secretary: I wouldn't be without mine now. I won't try and blind you with science, but I do know quite a bit about satellites. The technology's amazing – position can be pinpointed to within a metre. Of course, accuracy's down to the mapping companies who do the updating work, but new models come out all the time. It's entirely up to you of course, but imagine never having to ask for directions again!
Female: That'd be good – I'll certainly give it some thought!

[pause]

tone

Now you'll hear the recording again.

[The recording is repeated.]

[pause]

Extract 2 *You hear part of a discussion in which the anthropologist Paula Drew and the comedian Mike Morton are talking about their lives. Now look at questions three and four.*

[pause]

tone

Paula: We both grew up in a fairly rough part of the city, Mike, so I'm assuming you used comedy to keep yourself safe – and popular in the long run!
Mike: Well, in school, as you know, if you could run fast or make people laugh, you had a very good chance of surviving and emerging unscathed. I wasn't a fast runner, so I exploited comedy to avoid unwelcome attention. It seemed to come easy, and it worked.
Paula: Your type of comedy is less spontaneous than reflective. You see things from your own point of view, don't you, and create a world for other people to see. Whereas I explore the world that's already there, which most people don't see.
Mike: Don't you think that the key to achieving what you want in life is the realisation that it's going to be tough, and the sheer persistence that gets you there in the end?
Paula: What you have to have is massive self-confidence. With that you can do anything.
Mike: And being specific about what it is you want to do.
Paula: Ah well, that goes without saying.

[pause]

tone

Now you'll hear the recording again.

[The recording is repeated.]

[pause]

Extract 3 *You hear part of a radio discussion about holiday reading. Now look at questions five and six.*

[pause]

tone

Female: If you're English, a nice sad nineteenth-century romance is very useful if you're on holiday and you get attacked by homesickness because it conjures up dripping English autumn days perfectly.

Male: I always take something by this chap who's written a number of books about the criminal underworld of Boston, Massachusetts, which is hardly culturally or geographically a place that I know, but I find it fascinating. There's no doubt about it if you compile, as I do, dictionaries of slang for a living, one is drawn inevitably not alas to the great classics, who are on the whole rather light on slang, but to someone like this fellow who has this amazing ability, far beyond quoting, of writing 20 or 40 pages of dialogue in almost incomprehensible slang, which I have the most wonderful time going through. I find it very alluring.

[pause]

tone

Now you'll here the recording again.

[The recording is repeated.]

[pause]

That's the end of Part One.
Now turn to Part Two.

[pause]

PART 2 *You'll hear a reporter called Ruth Sampson describing a visit she made to the Arctic Circle with a team of Canadian wildlife experts. For questions 7 to 14, complete the sentences.*

You now have forty-five seconds to look at Part Two.

[pause]

tone

Last year I found myself flying to the Arctic Circle with five biologists from the Canadian Wildlife Service. As our small plane descended towards a snow-covered runway, I looked out of the window at the frozen ocean below. I could see small holes in the ice, and, around them, lots of extraordinary little figures rather like ants. I was told they were seals, basking on the ice in the sun. Ten minutes after we'd landed, I had my first sighting of a wolf, which my eagle-eyed colleagues pointed out to me at least seven hundred metres away, and later on I was lucky enough to see a caribou with its huge antlers at much closer range.

At first sight, the Arctic seems to be a kind of desert, but there *are* plants and animals around – you just have to look around for them. You may find what's called an oasis – this is a little confined area with access to water, where vegetation can establish itself and provide nutrients for animals. Arctic plants have evolved to cope with this harsh environment, like the yellow Arctic poppy, which only has a tiny tuft of leaves visible, as the bulk of the plant – a network of roots – stays underground. Its leaves remain green all winter, so it can make the most of the short growing season.

The diversity of bird species decreases as you travel north, but there *are* birds which spend the winter here, and others that come back in the spring. Most of these birds get their nourishment from seeds, although a predator like the snowy owl feeds on small mammals called lemmings, and others do manage to find fish.

For accommodation, we had tents which looked just like the igloos the local Inuit people build out of ice, with little tunnels at the front, only ours were orange and made of nylon! And our only connection to the outside world was our radio link. You notice how light the snow cover is – it scatters with the wind, and there are hardly any deep drifts.

Apart from the cold, the main hazard is the wildlife, and I received a brief introduction on the correct action to take if a polar bear came to visit. There are other large animals, like the musk ox, but they seldom pose a threat. Another thing was that recording the team's descriptions of wildlife, which was my task, was incredibly difficult. The recorder itself was fine, but batteries just don't work in the cold, so I had to hold them inside my thick coat to keep them warm.

But on the whole I found . . .

[pause]

tone

Now you'll hear the recording again.

[The recording is repeated.]

[pause]

That's the end of Part Two.
Now turn to Part Three.

[pause]

PART 3

You'll hear a radio interview with the gardening experts Jed and Helena Stone. For questions 15 to 20, choose the answer (A, B, C or D) which fits best according to what you hear. You now have one minute to look at Part Three.

[pause]

tone

Interviewer: Jed Stone's best known now for his talents as a garden designer – but he and his wife Helena ran a highly successful jewellery business in the nineteen nineties, which brought them fame and high living. Then they lost it all and, some years later, bought a derelict house which they renovated and now together they've created a garden. They join me in the studio today. You do seem to do most things in partnership, like the jewellery business, but using Jed's name. Why's that? Helena?

Helena: Well, this is a bit of a bone of contention, actually. We have a friend in PR who said, 'You have a great name, Jed Stone. People would pay a fortune for such a good name.' But, sadly, at the time, it never crossed my mind that I wouldn't get the credit for what we do, and that does get to me sometimes – but, there again, I'm very bad at putting myself forward. People see Jed as a figurehead, which is fine, actually, because I don't enjoy being recognised or get any thrill out of that, whereas Jed loves it.

Interviewer: Is that right, Jed?

Jed: Obviously, I'd love to say, 'No, I don't,' but yeah, I do. Even as a child, I thought it must be marvellous to walk down a street and have people know who you were. Ironically, that's the worst of it now. It would be nice just to go and buy a paper without somebody saying something. But I suppose I do like being a public figure. It gives me a sense that I've done something people appreciate. It doesn't stop me doing anything, but it does modify how I do it.

Interviewer: But Helena, you did appear on our television screens briefly as a presenter on *The Travel Show*. That must have been a dream job, travelling around the world?

Helena: Actually, I thought I was being heroic taking that job. I'd actually rather have gone down a coal mine. It was ironic really, because Jed adores travelling, whilst I hate it. The timing was critical though; I mean, we were living in this derelict house. We'd knocked huge holes in the walls to make windows and we could hardly afford to get the job finished and I wanted to be there when it was done. So I genuinely didn't want to do the job they were offering, but I felt I had no choice because, apart from anything else, it would provide us with a reasonable income.

Interviewer: So what about this jewel garden? Did you have a clear idea of what you wanted to do when you bought the house?

Jed: Not at all. In fact, we were provoked into action. I was giving a lecture on gardening and I was including some snaps of our own wilderness to show what certain plants looked like. But these photos hadn't loaded onto my laptop properly, and you couldn't see a thing. So I started to make it all up – describing this jewel garden with magical colours – it came straight out of my imagination, it hadn't been a long-term plan or anything. Anyway, as soon as I'd finished, these journalists came rushing up saying, 'We must come and take pictures of your jewel garden.' And I heard myself replying, 'Fine, but come when the colours are good, don't come now.' To cut a long story short, we had to make the jewel garden before they came, and actually, we did ninety per cent of the work that summer. That was our incentive!

Test 2 Key

Interviewer:	And why did you call it a 'jewel garden'? Having read about the disasters with the jewellery business, one would have thought you wouldn't want the word 'jewel' in your house at all.
Helena:	Well, I like to work on projects and if you have a project where you're thinking only of jewel colours then that starts to limit you, and design is all about reduction. Really it was just a good, positive way of tackling what plants we were putting in, and the way we were going to design the garden, wasn't it, Jed?
Jed:	Yeah. But for me it was also partly a metaphor, it's making something worthwhile out of a failure. We did spend years doing the jewellery and it wasn't all disastrous; there were good things about it too and we wanted to salvage them and treasure them. It seemed a waste not to take that bit of our lives and to somehow incorporate it into our new design venture – to take the bad experience and use it in a creative way.
Interviewer:	Jed and Helena, thank you for telling us about it today.

[pause]

tone

Now you'll hear the recording again.

[The recording is repeated.]

[pause]

That's the end of Part Three.
Now turn to Part Four.

[pause]

PART 4   *Part Four consists of two tasks. You'll hear five short extracts in which people are talking about weekend activities. Look at Task One. For questions 21 to 25, choose from the list A to H the activity each speaker is describing. Now look at Task Two. For questions 26 to 30, choose from the list A to H what each speaker felt about their activity. While you listen you must complete both tasks. You now have forty-five seconds to look at Part Four.*

[pause]

tone

Speaker One:	Well, we got there late unfortunately. The problem was that Dave couldn't find a parking space anywhere. We drove around for ages. I don't think we realised just how popular it was going to be. We nearly didn't bother, you know. Last month's was such a disappointment – there wasn't much to see and not many people turned up. But this time it was the complete opposite. There were all kinds of food, a huge fish section, clothes, miscellaneous stalls with goodness knows what. Apart from it being almost impossible to make progress past the stalls we quite enjoyed it.

[pause]

Test 2 Key

Speaker Two: Yes, Pete and I go quite regularly now. He wasn't too keen to begin with but over the last few months we've both got completely hooked. However, we were a bit unlucky last weekend. We were expecting great things and we'd been looking forward to it for ages. This was going to be the big one. We set off early, got the gear ready the night before, but after a couple of hours the weather set in. Couldn't see a thing. The visibility was down to about ten metres. There was no way we were going to reach the summit so we just had to abandon it. Discovered we'd lost one of our ropes when we got back home, just to cap it all.

[pause]

Speaker Three: I haven't been for ages. It was a real treat for me. Of course, before I was married I used to go several times a year, but I don't think I've been now since nineteen ninety-four. It's not that my wife objects to it, it's just, well, I don't know. I suppose I feel a bit guilty going off at the weekend. But it's good fun – I love seeing all the big names. Mind you, not a lot happened. Nothing to clap or cheer about, but it didn't seem to matter. It was just being there, encouraging the players and despairing when they got it all wrong.

[pause]

Speaker Four: We felt it was a good opportunity to celebrate. Occasions like this don't happen every day and everyone was in a good mood so we thought, 'Why not'? The thing is, we wanted it to be different, something that we'd always remember, something to round off a perfect day. Jamie had heard about this interesting place by the harbour where you sat on cushions and you prepared your own dishes. It sounded different so we set off for there. When we arrived, the manager had already heard about our success and even though he was busy, he still managed to find plenty of room for us all.

[pause]

Speaker Five: I was on my own at the weekend and I suppose I was a bit restless. You know, I've been working hard recently. I needed to get out in the fresh air and so I just headed off into the country. It was great – a beautiful day. It reminded me of when my father used to take me fishing. Well, I fancied a quick dip and so, as no one was around, I just stripped off and plunged in. It was marvellous, but I got a bit over-ambitious. Before I knew it, I was more than a mile out. It took me a very long time to get back and when I reached the shore again I lay in the sun for ages to get my breath back.

[pause]

tone

Now you'll hear the recording again.

[The recording is repeated.]

[pause]

That's the end of Part Four.

Test 2 Key

*There'll now be a pause of **five minutes** for you to **copy your answers onto the separate answer sheet**. Be sure to follow the numbering of all the questions. I'll remind you when there's one minute left, so that you're sure to finish in time.*

[Teacher, pause the recording here for five minutes. Remind your students when they have one minute left.]

That's the end of the test. Please stop now. Your supervisor will now collect all the question papers and answer sheets.

Test 3 Key

Paper 1 Reading (1 hour 15 minutes)

Part 1

1 A 2 D 3 B 4 A 5 B 6 B

Part 2

7 D 8 G 9 F 10 A 11 B 12 E

Part 3

13 D 14 B 15 B 16 C 17 B 18 A 19 A

Part 4

20 C/D 21 D/C 22 D 23 E 24 A 25 B 26 A 27 A/C 28 C/A
29 B/E 30 E/B 31 D 32 A/C 33 C/A 34 B

Paper 2 Writing (1 hour 30 minutes)

Task-specific Mark Schemes

Part 1

Question 1

Content (points covered)
For Band 3 or above, the candidate's **proposal** must:
- outline what the programme should include
- explain why
- explain why candidate's ideas would work best.

Organisation and cohesion
Clearly organised, headings an advantage.

Range
Language of description, explanation and persuasion.

Appropriacy of register and format
Formal to unmarked. Must be consistent.

Target reader
Would be informed.

Part 2

Question 2

Content (points covered)
For Band 3 or above, the candidate's **article** must:
- name a representative of their country, (fictional/legendary character would be acceptable)
- explain why s/he attracts attention
- give an opinion about the person's image.

Organisation and cohesion
Clear organisation with appropriate paragraphing.

Range
Language of description, opinion.

Appropriacy of register and format
Any, as long as consistent.

Target reader
Would know who the representative was and why they were famous.

Question 3

Content (points covered)
For Band 3 or above, the candidate's **information sheet** must:
- describe the possible danger(s) of an unhealthy lifestyle
- persuade the target reader(s) that living (more) healthily can be enjoyable
- give advice related to a healthy lifestyle.

Stronger candidates are likely to outline the dangers in a reassuring manner.

Organisation and cohesion
Clear organisation with appropriate paragraphing, using some linking devices. Use of bullets/headers may be an advantage.

Range
Language of description, advice, warning and persuasion.
Vocabulary related to food/nutrition and health/fitness.

Appropriacy of register and format
Unmarked or informal.

Target reader
Would be informed and consider the advice.

Question 4

Content (points covered)
For Band 3 or above, the candidate's **report** must:
- describe changes in attitude to at least one job/employment in general
- explain the reason for these changes in attitude
- predict possible future changes.

Organisation and cohesion
Report format. Headings an advantage. Clearly organised into paragraphs. Memo format acceptable.

Range
Vocabulary associated with work. Language of evaluation.

Appropriacy of register and format
Consistently formal or unmarked.

Target reader
Would be informed.

Question 5 (a)

Content (points covered)
For Band 3 or above, the candidate's **review** must:
- state which group of people the story is most likely to appeal to
- give reasons for the candidate's opinions.

Organisation and cohesion
Clearly organised into paragraphs with appropriate linking devices.

Range
Language of description, opinion and explanation.
Vocabulary related to description of and comment on a story.

Appropriacy of register and format
May mix registers if appropriate to approach taken by candidate.

Target reader
Would be informed.

Question 5 (b)

Content (points covered)
For Band 3 or above, the candidate's **article** must:
- comment on whether the candidate feels the story would make a good film or not
- explain whether the English, the Australian or the New Zealand scenes would provide the most interesting part of the film.

Organisation and cohesion
Clearly organised into paragraphs with appropriate linking devices.

Range
Language of description, opinion and explanation.
Vocabulary related to description of novels / films and comment on a story.

Appropriacy of register and format
May mix registers if appropriate to approach taken by candidate.

Target reader
Would be informed.

Paper 3   Use of English (1 hour)

Part 1
1 B   2 A   3 B   4 C   5 B   6 D   7 C   8 A   9 D   10 B   11 B
12 C

Part 2
13 where   14 this   15 whose   16 them/these   17 which   18 becoming/getting
19 despite   20 everything/anything/whatever   21 for   22 addition   23 all   24 One
25 off/from/on   26 with   27 themselves

Part 3
28 inseparably   29 increasingly   30 similarities   31 central   32 capability   33 expanse
34 sight   35 unavoidable   36 collision   37 proof

Part 4
38 turn   39 pour   40 short   41 line   42 production

Part 5
43 took | (any/much) notice of   44 seeing him onstage | that made   45 it is/can be to | come up
46 is highly | thought/spoken   47 a matter of time | before   48 to everyone | because as many
49 with | a discussion on/of/about OR by holding/having | a discussion on/of/about   50 in | no doubt OR not in | any doubt

Test 3 Key

Paper 4 Listening (approximately 40 minutes)

Part 1
1 C   2 B   3 A   4 C   5 B   6 A

Part 2
7 age groups   8 (university) student   9 heights   10 websites   11 helmet   12 2,000
13 airport   14 several months

Part 3
15 C   16 B   17 D   18 A   19 B   20 B

Part 4
21 G   22 F   23 E   24 A   25 H   26 D   27 F   28 H   29 E   30 B

Transcript	This is the Cambridge Certificate in Advanced English Listening Test. Test Three.
	I'm going to give you the instructions for this test. I'll introduce each part of the test and give you time to look at the questions.
	At the start of each piece you'll hear this sound:
	tone
	You'll hear each piece twice.
	Remember, while you're listening, write your answers on the **question paper**. You'll have five minutes at the end of the test to **copy your answers onto the separate answer sheet**.
	There'll now be a pause. Please ask any questions now, because you must not speak during the test.
	[pause]
PART 1	Now open your question paper and look at Part One.
	[pause]
	You'll hear three different extracts. For questions one to six, choose the answer (A, B or C) which fits best according to what you hear. There are two questions for each extract.
Extract 1	You overhear a man telling a friend about a trip to the theatre. Now look at questions one and two.
	[pause]

158

Test 3 Key

tone

Woman: So, did you go to that play in the end?
Man: I did, and it was an interesting experience.
Woman: Really? Why's that?
Man: Well, for a start, the theatre was in Pelham Street. Now I've walked up and down that street many times, but I never realised there was a theatre there.
Woman: No, nor had I. Has it always been there?
Man: Apparently. Anyway, it took a bit of finding; you go through a doorway, down a passage – you know the sort of place. And when you do get inside, it's really surprisingly intimate – I shouldn't think it holds more than about forty people.
Woman: And the play?
Man: Well, the show was a big success up in London last year – huge audiences – but unfortunately only a handful of people turned up for last night's performance. I'm not surprised though – it was rather amateurish. They could have done with using at least a bit of make-up and learning their parts better. They just about managed to cover up their mistakes by really throwing themselves into their characters.
Woman: Yes, I know what you mean.

[pause]

tone

Now you'll hear the recording again.

[The recording is repeated.]

[pause]

Extract 2 *You hear a media interview with a tour operator at a conference on what is called 'responsible' tourism. Now look at questions three and four.*

[pause]

tone

Reporter: Excuse me, sir, could you spare a couple of minutes before the conference to answer some questions?
Man: Well, if you could make it really brief.
Reporter: You're always identified with 'responsible' tourism – how do you feel it's different from normal tourism?
Man: Our trips have unique themes including culinary, spa, angling, indigenous peoples – plus those specially designed for groups with special needs. But it's the tour *organisation* that really differentiates them from others. Take the Himalayas: several of our outdoor staff work only six months of the season but are well paid all year round. Then we always use solar-powered equipment and make our environmental commitment known to every tourist . . .
Reporter: Do you believe people are willing to pay more for your kind of tourism?

159

Man: Not in the main, but I think they will be once their thinking is revolutionised: they just become aware of the global consequences of the choices they make. Then I think they'll see that the future of the world depends on justice in commerce and industry and they'll dig deep in their pockets – I must rush now, but come to my session!

[pause]

tone

Now you'll hear the recording again.

[The recording is repeated.]

[pause]

Extract 3

You hear two local radio presenters, Laura and Steve, talking about a forthcoming rugby match. Now look at questions five and six.

[pause]

tone

Laura: So, Steve, what about next week's all-important match in Melbourne – Australia versus Wales? The teams are pretty evenly matched, aren't they?

Steve: Australia are certainly the favourites, but whether they'll pull it off and by what margin is anybody's guess.

Laura: A real cliff-hanger probably. And there's huge interest in this match, but I understand the Welsh supporters haven't been allowed enough tickets.

Steve: As usual, the authorities *have* given priority to the home fans, but that seems eminently reasonable to me.

Laura: There's concern, isn't there, about two of the Welsh players who are currently recovering from injuries?

Steve: Yes, and there's still doubt about whether they'll play, but even if they don't, I reckon it'll be a gripping match to watch. And to anybody listening who's lucky enough to have tickets, Melbourne's filling up with school groups and junior teams because the Australians are very keen to encourage their youngsters to take up rugby, so better make sure you book somewhere to stay right now. And, of course, you could consider becoming a member of the Welsh team's fan club, although it's a bit late to take advantage of their cheap flight deals.

Laura: Well, thanks for that, Steve.

[pause]

tone

Now you'll hear the recording again.

[The recording is repeated.]

[pause]

That's the end of Part One.
Now turn to Part Two.

[pause]

PART 2

You'll hear a woman called Kate Assadi talking to a group of people interested in taking up skydiving. For questions 7 to 14, complete the sentences.

You now have forty-five seconds to look at Part Two.

[pause]

tone

Hello! I'm Kate Assadi, and I'm here to talk about my hobby, which is skydiving. So why do people want to jump out of a plane? In the UK, this is still seen as something done by crazy young people! But in the USA, skydiving is a hobby that has been taken up by people from all age groups, by anyone looking for excitement, from twenty-year-olds to people enjoying an active retirement.

I wanted to do skydiving as a teenager, but my parents weren't very keen on the idea, and wouldn't give their permission. So, my first jump was as a university student – when I was able to get a discount. Immediately, I was hooked! I couldn't afford to do it regularly though, until I started working as a lawyer.

Why do I do it? Well, skydiving makes you feel great – you forget all your problems. There aren't really any health benefits, although I know several business executives with stressful jobs who do skydiving to help them relax. Of course, some people start skydiving to help them get over a fear of heights. If they can face up to their fear – and jump out of a plane at a height of three thousand metres, it helps them to build up the confidence to tackle other things.

So, how do you start? The equipment for skydiving is specialised, and not easy to get in local sports shops. Nowadays, most people buy skydiving kit from websites – there's more choice and you can see photographs. Though when you're buying second-hand on the internet, you should ask to see the equipment first. I got my skydiving camera that way and last week I got a helmet with a fifty per cent discount. You need a good helmet by the way – it's the most important part of your equipment.

For your first skydive, you jump from a height of over three thousand metres – strapped to an instructor who's required to have done at least two thousand jumps before. You dive down in free fall, for thirty seconds . . . And when the parachute opens, you float down sedately – landing very gently! After that, most people can't wait to have another go!

Still nervous? – Don't worry! All trainee skydivers must wear an appliance known as the 'automatic parachute' – it's compulsory – so even if you black out, your parachute will still open on its own. These rules are for safety reasons. So . . . what's stopping you?

If you're interested, you need to get in touch with the Parachute Association, and you'll find the contact details through your local airport. They'll give advice on how to get started. You can learn to skydive over a weekend, but I suggest the best way is to do it over several months – that allows you to build up your confidence gradually. Skydiving's great. It'll give you a whole new outlook on life!

Test 3 Key

[pause]

tone

Now you'll hear the recording again.

[The recording is repeated.]

[pause]

That's the end of Part Two.
Now turn to Part Three.

[pause]

PART 3   *You'll hear an interview with an engineer called Roger Moffat, who now works in the film industry. For questions 15 to 20, choose the answer (A, B, C or D) which fits best according to what you hear. You now have one minute to look at Part Three.*

[pause]

tone

Interviewer: It seems only fitting that former construction engineer Roger Moffat should've used his redundancy money to change direction and break into Hollywood, creating special effects for film and television. For, by his own flamboyant admission, he's no conventional engineer, but a born performer who loves an audience. Do you remember a certain car commercial in which the car was driven down the side of a skyscraper? The building façade and windows were built by Roger's own company for a daring stunt whose trade secret he will not divulge. He also constructed sections of a bridge for the film *Mary Reilly*, which starred Julia Roberts and John Malkovich. So, Roger, how did it all start?

Roger Moffat: Well, about ten years ago I had a heart by-pass operation and about the same time I was made redundant. I was feeling pretty low at the time, so I decided that the only thing to do was to take my working life into my own hands and set up my own business.

Interviewer: And what kind of success did you have in the early days?

Roger Moffat: You could say it was a bit like taking a rollercoaster ride and wondering when you were going to come flying off at break-neck speed! Everything was a challenge: finance, production, marketing.

Interviewer: But that's all in the past, you're . . . you're apparently much sought after now. I hear forthcoming film productions are queuing up for your services.

Roger Moffat: Some – yes. There's no doubt that we're certainly growing rapidly but we're still small, and I think it's probably important to remain that way. I've seen too many organisations just grow and grow and in the end they finish up over-reaching themselves – stretching themselves to the limit.

Interviewer: Do you have any regrets about the way things have gone? About the way your life has taken a different turn?

Roger Moffat: To be honest, none at all. I feel that I've escaped being a slave to a regular income, from commuting, from having to justify my actions to everyone, from having to attend the office party, from having to book my holidays in advance –

	actually, I don't have any holidays at all at the moment, come to think of it. I'm too busy! But best of all, I've nothing to do with office politics!
Interviewer:	Probably the biggest advantage of all! So, what's the secret of your meteoric rise?
Roger Moffat:	Oh, I couldn't have done anything without the support of my wife, Lili, who's also my business partner, and there's our two daughters, of course, Natasha and Katia. They've all been wonderful.
Interviewer:	So what kind of job did you start out doing?
Roger Moffat:	I graduated in mechanical engineering and then spent about twenty years in industry. Then my job – I was the chief engineer in an air-conditioning firm – just disappeared overnight. Anyway, after that, I set up my own computer-aided system that makes really intricate architectural models.
Interviewer:	And you also supply components for the aerospace industry, don't you?
Roger Moffat:	We do, but I have to admit that it's the film work that really interests me most.
Interviewer:	Do you worry about the future?
Roger Moffat:	No more than anyone else. I mean, there's no job security anywhere these days, is there? Of course, it's a risk running your own company, but then you're equally as vulnerable staying employed. I decided it was safer to be in charge of my own show than to be a part of someone else's. Naturally, I've had problems. We had to sell the family house, the one I built myself. But, looking back, it all seems worth it. I was always infuriated by having to justify myself to people whom I didn't consider to be my intellectual superiors!
Interviewer:	How would you describe yourself? What are your strengths, weaknesses?
Roger Moffat:	I think I'm a bit of an oddball character really. I suppose you might say that I was a hard-headed romantic. I believe that an engineer has to invent ideas. You need to be very talented. You need to have a feeling for balance and form. You also need to feel you have status and that people value what you're doing. I've always seen engineers as sort of visionaries, if you like. Engineering can give you great power, a position in the world and, if you don't look after your engineers, then you're in great danger of losing your prestige, your position. Engineering's still the 'workshop of the world' in every country. We've built superb ships, motorbikes, motor cars. Now we're entering a new phase with new challenges.
Interviewer:	And what about the tools of your trade? How do you view those?
Roger Moffat:	To me, mechanical things are magical: a motor car is a thrilling bit of science. The microchip is a masterpiece of theoretical design; machines of unbelievable complexity make them. But from my point of view, the most rewarding thing of all is that all these things are designed by engineers.
Interviewer:	You certainly seem to have a passion for your profession. I think the mystique of the film world will be pretty safe in your hands. Thanks for coming to talk to us today, Roger.

[pause]

tone

Now you'll hear the recording again.

Test 3 Key

[The recording is repeated.]

[pause]

That's the end of Part Three.
Now turn to Part Four.

[pause]

PART 4   *Part Four consists of two tasks. You'll hear five short extracts in which people are talking about the importance of eating breakfast. Look at Task One. For questions 21 to 25, choose from the list A to H each speaker's occupation. Now look at Task Two. For questions 26 to 30, choose from the list A to H what each speaker says. While you listen you must complete both tasks. You now have forty-five seconds to look at Part Four.*

[pause]

tone

Speaker One: In common with most of my colleagues on the track, I'm training in the morning most of the time, as well as throughout the day. And sometimes we have to compete in the mornings too, as early as seven or eight in some places in the world. And people say to me, 'And you really eat before that?' But, if you think about it, you absolutely can't perform to the best of your abilities without fuelling your body – or your mind for that matter. So, the message for kids who've got their sights set on gold is, 'Don't skip your breakfast before you train.'

[pause]

Speaker Two: I have to admit that I was one of those awful people who used to tell others to do something that I didn't do myself. It wasn't until I was invited to present a report on a conference in the USA, and I was sceptical before that too, that I came back a convert. There's good research to show that people are healthier if they eat breakfast, and everything I heard was quite convincing and I've gone on to use quite a lot of it in my column – you know, I read up the research and did a few pieces on it myself, which were quite well received, even by the professionals.

[pause]

Speaker Three: Well, I read that the latest thinking is that whatever you eat in the morning, your metabolic rate goes up slightly, so the rate you burn calories goes up too. Even if you sit about a lot like me, if you've had a good breakfast, you still won't necessarily put on weight. Sounds crazy. But just think: if you don't eat first thing, you get a rumbly tummy about mid-morning, and what happens next? Well, what I do is rush out to the vending machine after I've pulled into the next station and grab something quick, which is usually chocolate or crisps – you know, something full of fat and sugar! So I suppose those newspaper articles are right really, aren't they?

[pause]

Speaker Four: I'll be absolutely honest with you – I usually wake up and don't feel particularly hungry, especially when you've got an early start. And you can't be absolutely sure where the next meal is coming from – I mean it could be breakfast, lunch or dinner, depending on where your next stopover is and what time it is there. And during all that time you might have served all manner of meals too, so you have to think ahead and I generally make sure I have something breakfast-like before each shift, even if it's not morning, and then I don't get hunger pangs in the cabin.

[pause]

Speaker Five: I think that if you're someone who 'skips' breakfast, for want of a better term, you don't know what you're missing until you try. And I think that it's especially important to try and get this message across to parents. I can tell which ones in my group have missed breakfast: they lack energy and they're the ones who get all the colds and that, honestly. But it's got to fit in with the whole family's normal way of life too. It's no good making great resolutions and breaking them two days later because you can't get up in time or it's going to make you late for work.

[pause]

tone

Now you'll hear the recording again.

[The recording is repeated.]

[pause]

That's the end of Part Four.

*There'll now be a pause of **five minutes** for you to **copy your answers onto the separate answer sheet**. Be sure to follow the numbering of all the questions. I'll remind you when there's one minute left, so that you're sure to finish in time.*

[Teacher, pause the recording here for five minutes. Remind your students when they have one minute left.]

That's the end of the test. Please stop now. Your supervisor will now collect all the question papers and answer sheets.

Test 4 Key

Paper 1   Reading (1 hour 15 minutes)

Part 1
1 D   2 C   3 A   4 B   5 B   6 D

Part 2
7 E   8 A   9 G   10 C   11 D   12 B

Part 3
13 A   14 D   15 B   16 C   17 B   18 A   19 D

Part 4
20 F   21 A   22 C   23 E   24 A   25 E   26 D   27 B   28 F   29 B
30 C   31 C   32 D   33 E   34 E

Paper 2   Writing (1 hour 30 minutes)

Task-specific Mark Schemes

Part 1

Question 1

Content (points covered)
For Band 3 or above, the candidate's **letter** must:
- say what is good
- explain what they are dissatisfied with
- suggest improvement to services.

Organisation and cohesion
Clearly organised, with appropriate opening and closing formulae.

Range
Language of description and suggestion.

Appropriacy of register and format
Formal or unmarked.

Target reader
Would be informed.

Part 2

Question 2

Content (points covered)
For Band 3 or above, the candidate's **review** must:
- describe and identify **two** games/series of games
- describe graphics/visuals

Test 4 Key

- discuss appeal of the games
- discuss value for money.

Organisation and cohesion
Clear organisation with appropriate paragraphing. Letter format acceptable.

Range
Language of description and evaluation. Vocabulary of games/computers.

Appropriacy of register and format
Any, as long as consistent.

Target reader
Would be informed about the two games.

Question 3

Content (points covered)
For Band 3 or above, the candidate's **entry** must:
- refer to a particular place and time (**NB** This could be the very recent or very distant past.)
- describe possible experiences
- explain reasons for this choice.

Organisation and cohesion
Clear paragraphing. May be article or narrative format.

Range
Language of description and evaluation. Vocabulary specific to the place and time.

Appropriacy of register and format
Any, as long as consistent.

Target reader
Would have a clear picture of the time and place described and understand the reasons for the choice.

Question 4

Content (points covered)
For a Band 3 or above, the candidate's **article** must:
- suggest how best to prepare for a driving test
- give advice about what readers should and/or should not do on the day itself.

Organisation and cohesion
Clear organisation with appropriate paragraphing.

Range
Language of advice and suggestion. Vocabulary related to cars and driving.

Appropriacy of register and format
Any, as long as consistent.

Target reader
Would be informed.

Question 5 (a)

Content (points covered)
For Band 3 or above, the candidate's **essay** must:
- describe the picture of life in rural Virginia given in the story
- explain why the candidate would or would not like to have been brought up in such a place.

Test 4 Key

Organisation and cohesion
Clearly organised into paragraphs with appropriate linking devices.

Range
Language of description, opinion and explanation.
Vocabulary related to description of setting and comment on a story.

Appropriacy of register and format
Formal to unmarked. Must be consistent.

Target reader
Would be informed.

Question 5 (b)

Content (points covered)
For Band 3 or above, the candidate's **report** must:
- briefly describe the story
- explain why it would or would not be a good choice for students who want to practise their English through a Book Club.

Organisation and cohesion
Clearly organised into paragraphs with appropriate linking devices.

Range
Language of description, opinion and explanation.
Vocabulary related to description of plot and comment on a story.

Appropriacy of register and format
Formal to unmarked. Must be consistent.

Target reader
Would be informed.

Paper 3   Use of English (1 hour)

Part 1
1 D   2 C   3 B   4 D   5 A   6 B   7 D   8 B   9 B   10 D   11 C
12 A

Part 2
13 for   14 into   15 its   16 to   17 which/that   18 with   19 From   20 a
21 came   22 our   23 by   24 enough   25 did   26 all   27 had

Part 3
28 impressive   29 worldwide   30 safety   31 effectively   32 losses   33 enthusiasts
34 unsuccessful   35 strengthen   36 improvements   37 pressure

Part 4
38 landed   39 run   40 expression   41 treated   42 mark

Part 5
43 have any | recollection (at all) of   44 made/gotten a name | for   45 count on | being
46 to put up with | (any) rudeness   47 can afford this/the holiday | as/so long   48 no chance | of winning
49 on the point | of leaving   50 made it | impossible for

168

Paper 4 Listening (approximately 40 minutes)

Part 1
1 A   2 C   3 C   4 B   5 C   6 B

Part 2
7 Greeks   8 design   9 public libraries   10 time, motivation (in either order)
11 weekend workshop   12 puzzles   13 soap dishes   14 chests of drawers

Part 3
15 B   16 A   17 B   18 B   19 C   20 D

Part 4
21 B   22 G   23 C   24 E   25 F   26 D   27 A   28 F   29 C   30 B

Transcript

This is is the Cambridge Certificate in Advanced English Listening Test. Test Four.

I'm going to give you the instructions for this test. I'll introduce each part of the test and give you time to look at the questions.

At the start of each piece you'll hear this sound:

tone

You'll hear each piece twice.

Remember, while you're listening, write your answers on the **question paper**. You'll have five minutes at the end of the test to **copy your answers** onto the **separate answer sheet**.

There'll now be a pause. Please ask any questions now, because you must not speak during the test.

[pause]

PART 1

Now open your question paper and look at Part One.

[pause]

You'll hear three different extracts. For questions one to six, choose the answer (A, B or C) which fits best according to what you hear. There are two questions for each extract.

Extract 1

You hear part of an interview with a broadcaster who is talking about a series of programmes he presented about landscape painting. Now look at questions one and two.

[pause]

tone

Test 4 Key

Interviewer: Why did you decide to include a painting by a famous politician?
Man: I wanted to remind viewers that amateur painting has its own purpose, that scores and scores of people paint for themselves as that politician did. And I liked his daughter's explanation that it helped to give him some respite from the pressures of public life. I thought that was important to focus on, so that we weren't just talking about painters as professionals who had really cracked it and who taught us things about their technique.
Interviewer: You draw yourself, don't you?
Man: Yes, I've always liked it though I'm afraid my attempts aren't very good, so I keep them purely for my own amusement. The intensity of drawing is always a great thrill. I can't say it's a relief, which it obviously is for some people. You have to use your eyes to look more carefully at a scene than you would if you were just out for a walk, or even if you were taking a photograph as an amateur. There's something about drawing that forces you to see things and think about them.

[pause]

tone

Now you'll hear the recording again.

[The recording is repeated.]

[pause]

Extract 2

You hear an amateur pilot called Gina Nesbit talking about doing aerobatics in her small plane. Now look at questions three and four.

[pause]

tone

Interviewer: I've only ever been up in a plane once where the pilot turned the plane over in an aerobatic display and I've never been more scared or felt sicker. Do you get that sinking feeling too, Gina?
Gina: I'm very fortunate in that I don't. This came as a pleasant surprise to me because I do get terribly seasick. I find that what is routine and what I'm used to doing isn't frightening. Learning some of the new manoeuvres, though, can be quite daunting because this is a single-seater plane. So, the first time I do anything new, I'm on my own except for the guidance of my coach, who's on the ground.
Interviewer: What's the real thrill for you of performing these difficult manoeuvres in competitions?
Gina: It's exciting of course, but ultimately the reward comes from knowing that you've done it with precision. It involves an unusual combination of mental preparation, physical preparation and skill. It's not as difficult as you might first think to fly the sequences of movements. What *is* difficult is doing it to a high enough standard to avoid the faults the judges are looking out for.

[pause]

Test 4 Key

tone

Now you'll hear the recording again.

[The recording is repeated.]

[pause]

Extract 3   *You overhear a chef called George talking to a friend about his daily routine. Now look at questions five and six.*

[pause]

tone

Fran: I'm exhausted. It took an hour to drive five kilometres!
George: You should do what I do and use a motorbike.
Fran: Is it much quicker?
George: It is a bit, because you avoid some queues. The great thing is, when I put on my helmet, I'm shut away, you know, in my own little world and that means I arrive feeling quite calm. I started riding a motorbike where I grew up in the country because there weren't any buses.
Fran: So is that your most prized possession? I was asked recently what my favourite thing at home was. As a chef I imagine yours is something in the kitchen, your cooker perhaps.
George: The one at the restaurant is fantastic because it was specially designed for me. It's hard to say here. My family love the kitchen table, where they chat for hours. Given the late hours I work, I hardly participate in that. No, my workplace is so hot and sticky that what I long for is a shower when I get home. I feel the stresses of the day disappear with the water. Odd thing to choose, isn't it?

[pause]

tone

Now you'll hear the recording again.

[The recording is repeated.]

[pause]

*That's the end of Part One.
Now turn to Part Two.*

[pause]

PART 2   *You'll hear an art teacher called Rosa Weston giving a talk about making mosaics – works of art that are made out of small pieces of glass and stone. For questions 7 to 14, complete the sentences. You now have forty-five seconds to look at Part Two.*

Test 4 Key

[pause]

tone

I'd been teaching art for about ten years when I went on holiday to Greece. While I was there, I became really interested in the art of making mosaics and decided to include this in the courses I run. Many people assume that the Romans invented mosaic, but it was the Greeks who were the true craftsmen. And they, in turn, probably picked it up from the Sumerians. But it was the Romans who brought mosaics to Britain. And, apart from the introduction of nylon backing to hold the tiles together, the techniques themselves haven't changed much over five thousand years. It's the designs which have undergone a really radical change. In the recent past, modern mosaics have been restricted to the walls of public libraries and the odd swimming pool, and, by and large, it looked as if the true art of the mosaic could well disappear. Fortunately, that has not happened.

People often ask me why I prefer to spend hours teaching my students to stick tiny squares onto tiles when I could be doing something else. And it's certainly the case that the process demands both time and motivation on occasions. It can even give you a really bad headache! But, in fact, there's something very therapeutic about it. I think it has something to do with breaking things up and then reconstructing them.

For every course I teach, we have jars and jars of brightly coloured glass, odd bits of china, broken plates and dishes, and most people just can't wait to start sticking them onto larger stretches of concrete. For the beginners, we produce mosaic packs, which contain all the essentials you need and explain clearly how to go about things. Each course includes a weekend workshop, which is attended by the majority of students, and it's actually a wonderful way of relaxing. I'm often asked if I do puzzles, and it's not such a silly question as it sounds because it's a very good comparison of skills. Some people do get a bit scared, faced with all that choice, but that's why the mosaic packs are so popular. But I try to teach people to be inventive as well.

If you look around yourself, there's plenty of evidence that the art is enjoying a revival. Not only do you see mosaic ashtrays and soap dishes, but you can actually now find them decorating underground station walls. Now, I'm not suggesting that you start pulling your own home to pieces and replacing everything with mosaics, although I often find myself looking at chests of drawers and thinking, 'Hmm, just a border, perhaps!' Still, my reply to my over-anxious students is, 'All right, I know it takes hours, but, after all, it's a labour of love, and you have something which will give you pleasure for a long time afterwards.' Now if you're interested in trying out the effect in your own home . . .

[pause]

Now you'll hear the recording again.

tone

[The recording is repeated.]

[pause]

That's the end of Part Two.
Now turn to Part Three.

[pause]

PART 3

You'll hear part of a radio programme in which two people, Sally White and Martin Jones, are discussing the popularity of audio books. For questions 15 to 20, choose the answer (A, B, C or D) which fits best according to what you hear. You now have one minute to look at Part Three.

[pause]

tone

Interviewer: And today our subject for discussion is audio books. We have two guests in the studio – Martin Jones, who owns an audio bookshop, and Sally White, whose job it is to abridge – or shorten – books for the audio market. Now, I was amazed to find out just how popular it has become to listen to books on tape. What do you think is the reason for this, Sally?

Sally: Well, people are often very short of time. If you commute each day and have to spend, say, an hour in the car . . . then you can listen to part of a tape . . . and then go on where you left off. And many people like to listen to audio books while doing monotonous household chores, like ironing or dusting. However, I suspect that it's when people are trying to drop off at the end of a busy day that greatest use is made of them. I suppose it's like being read to as kids.

Interviewer: Yes, and in fact these audio books have also become popular among children. I often listen to them with mine. I suppose the fear here is that children will become lazy . . . I mean it's much easier to listen to a story than read it yourself.

Sally: Yes, of course it is, but I'm not sure this will necessarily put children off reading. I don't know . . . but the great thing is that they can listen to books which are far too difficult for them to read. It may mean, of course, that busy parents are tempted to put on a tape rather than take the time to read to their kids. But then, I'm sure many would actually prefer to listen to professionals rather than tired mums and dads . . .

Interviewer: What do you think, Martin?

Martin: Well, I'd like to tell you about a lady who came into this shop just last week . . . and she was telling us about these family driving holidays to France, which used to be a disaster with the kids in the back making a row, not being able to understand French radio. And she swore she would never take them to France again. Then she discovered audio books and suddenly the journeys there are a joy.

Interviewer: Now I hear that audio books are even more popular in the States . . .

Martin: Yes, it's certainly a huge, huge market in the States although I don't think audio books started there. Maybe it's because there's a tradition here in the UK from radio of spoken words being an acceptable medium, whereas in

Test 4 Key

	America, of course, it's a different story. In the main, Americans don't seem to get as much drama or stories on the radio, so they're going out and getting audio books. And the principal attraction is that they need something to listen to because of the time they spend on the road – places are so much farther apart. An audio book passes the time . . .
Interviewer:	And what are the reasons for sometimes asking the author to do the reading rather than employing a professional?
Sally:	It depends. Obviously the author is the one who's closest to the book and they may have a particular interpretation of the book that they are anxious to portray. Most authors will have already done public readings of their books anyway as part of their promotional activities at the time of publication, so they've probably read parts of it already. Otherwise, professional actors are used. We're very lucky in Britain to have such a wealth of actors who can bring the story alive completely.
Interviewer:	Now, Sally, your job is to abridge books especially for the audio market. I suspect a lot of people would say that you shouldn't mess about with what an author has written.
Sally:	No, I don't agree. Most of the abridgements these days are really extremely good. Abridgers interpret the story in the way they believe the author has written it. But the point about abridgements is that one's adapting it to create a new version of the story so it will inevitably be different to the original. Now, obviously some books are easier to abridge than others . . .
Interviewer:	Yes. I'd imagine a thousand-page volume by Charles Dickens must be a bit of a nightmare . . .
Sally:	Well, what we do is to trim the excess off so it's more to do with the way they write. Beryl Bainbridge, for instance, writes so beautifully and sparsely that it's harder to cut into her than Charles Dickens with his pages of detailed descriptions. This is probably the case with any kind of book.
Martin:	We shouldn't forget that many books are not abridged before being taped. I would say that these have now grown to account for about twenty per cent of the audio market. So, yes, some people do prefer to listen to the whole book. We've got *Anna Karenina* that has just come on the market. It's on twenty-four tapes – so, you can imagine how long it is!
Interviewer:	Twenty-four tapes? How long is a tape?
Martin:	Well, each tape is about ninety minutes and the whole set comes to ninety pounds. Though it's a lot of money, we're talking about a lifetime's listening, which is really something, isn't it?
Interviewer:	Well, thank you both very much . . . and now . . .

[pause]

Now you'll hear the recording again.

[The recording is repeated.]

[pause]

That's the end of Part Three.
Now turn to Part Four.

Test 4 Key

	[pause]
PART 4	*Part Four consists of two tasks. You'll hear five short extracts in which people are talking about starting a business. Look at Task One. For questions 21 to 25, choose from the list A to H the reason each speaker gives for starting a business. Now look at Task Two. For questions 26 to 30, choose from the list A to H the comment each speaker makes about their business. While you listen you must complete both tasks. You now have forty-five seconds to look at Part Four.*
	[pause]
	tone
Speaker One:	I'd never really considered starting my own business until last year. My friends were always on at me about what a good idea it would be, but I couldn't see the point. It wasn't as if I didn't have a good job – but then when there was talk about reducing the workforce, and I was offered a lot of money to leave, I thought, 'Why not try setting up on my own?' I suppose I realised that I really didn't have that much to lose. There were the usual initial problems of course, most of them financial, as I struggled to get things off the ground. But I don't regret my decision.
	[pause]
Speaker Two:	Although I know a lot of people are forced into this position through redundancy or whatever, in my case it all started when I fell out with my boss about a sales plan. He was so patronising and suddenly I felt I just couldn't take any more. Next day, I went back and handed in my resignation. The thought of having my own business had always been at the back of my mind, I suppose, and this seemed the perfect moment to go for it. My wife had mixed feelings at the time but she can hardly complain now – we've never been so well off and can now look forward to a comfortable retirement! It's such a relief not having someone looking over my shoulder the whole time.
	[pause]
Speaker Three:	My husband had always liked the idea of rural life, and when a job in a village school came up he felt it was a chance he couldn't miss. The move to the country was difficult for me, though, because it meant having to give up my position in a really good company. I could've commuted but it would have taken hours every day. There were no businesses like that in the area. So it was a case of setting up on my own or going into early retirement. I couldn't have managed without a computer and access to the Internet. I must admit that I miss my colleagues – but I make sure I see them if I'm in London.
	[pause]
Speaker Four:	The idea came to me after we'd had a lot of work done on our house. It left us really hard up and I found I was having to do a lot of the making good myself to keep costs down. Although I was a complete novice, friends who came

Test 4 Key

round commented on what a great job I'd done and kept on at me to do up *their* places. It was a bit of a leap in the dark because I was trained as a careers adviser, but I've managed to persuade a friend of mine who *does* have some experience to come in with me, and here we are with our own little decorating company. Although I've yet to make my fortune, every job brings a fresh set of challenges to overcome, which is something I never had before.

[pause]

Speaker Five: We've spent several years trying to bring up children and have careers at the same time, so we knew how little time working people had to do mundane jobs like making a dentist's appointment or cleaning the car. So when I read a feature about a company in the US which you could call to do these everyday tasks, I thought, 'What a brilliant idea!' Within a year we'd set up our own company and our feeling was right – there certainly is a great demand for this type of service in the UK as well. It shouldn't be long before we start making a real profit.

[pause]

Now you'll hear the recording again.

[The recording is repeated.]

[pause]

That's the end of Part Four.

*There'll now be a pause of **five minutes** for you to **copy your answers onto the separate answer sheet**. Be sure to follow the numbering of all the questions. I'll remind you when there's one minute left, so that you're sure to finish in time.*

[Teacher, pause the recording here for five minutes. Remind your students when they have one minute left.]

That's the end of the test. Please stop now. Your supervisor will now collect all the question papers and answer sheets.

Sample answer sheet: Paper 1

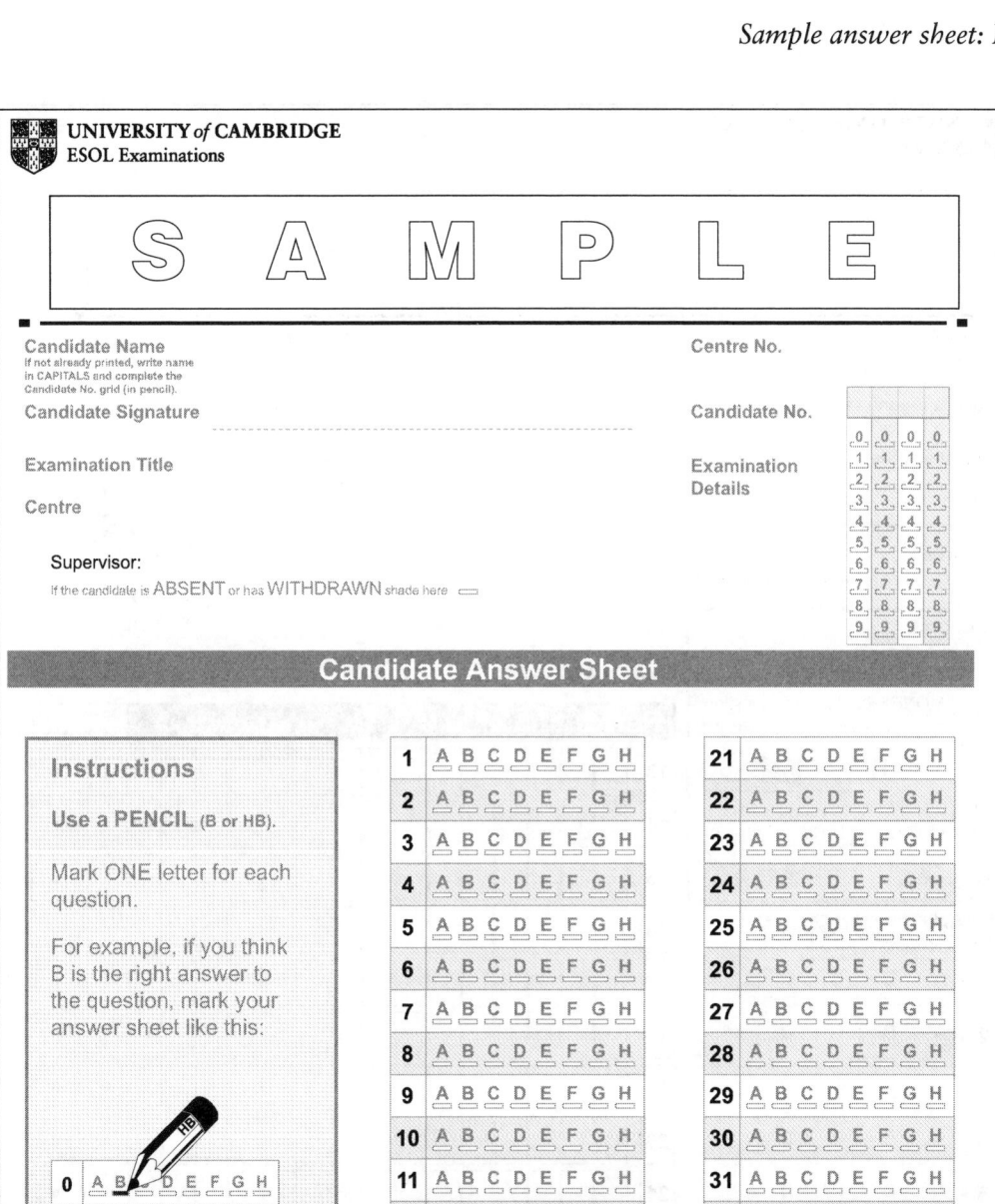

UNIVERSITY of CAMBRIDGE
ESOL Examinations

SAMPLE

Candidate Name
If not already printed, write name in CAPITALS and complete the Candidate No. grid (in pencil).

Candidate Signature

Examination Title

Centre

Supervisor:
If the candidate is ABSENT or has WITHDRAWN shade here ▭

Centre No.

Candidate No.

Examination Details

Candidate Answer Sheet

Instructions

Use a PENCIL (B or HB).

Mark ONE letter for each question.

For example, if you think B is the right answer to the question, mark your answer sheet like this:

0 A ■ C D E F G H

Rub out any answer you wish to change using an eraser.

1 A B C D E F G H	21 A B C D E F G H
2 A B C D E F G H	22 A B C D E F G H
3 A B C D E F G H	23 A B C D E F G H
4 A B C D E F G H	24 A B C D E F G H
5 A B C D E F G H	25 A B C D E F G H
6 A B C D E F G H	26 A B C D E F G H
7 A B C D E F G H	27 A B C D E F G H
8 A B C D E F G H	28 A B C D E F G H
9 A B C D E F G H	29 A B C D E F G H
10 A B C D E F G H	30 A B C D E F G H
11 A B C D E F G H	31 A B C D E F G H
12 A B C D E F G H	32 A B C D E F G H
13 A B C D E F G H	33 A B C D E F G H
14 A B C D E F G H	34 A B C D E F G H
15 A B C D E F G H	35 A B C D E F G H
16 A B C D E F G H	36 A B C D E F G H
17 A B C D E F G H	37 A B C D E F G H
18 A B C D E F G H	38 A B C D E F G H
19 A B C D E F G H	39 A B C D E F G H
20 A B C D E F G H	40 A B C D E F G H

© UCLES 2008 Photocopiable

Sample answer sheet: Paper 3

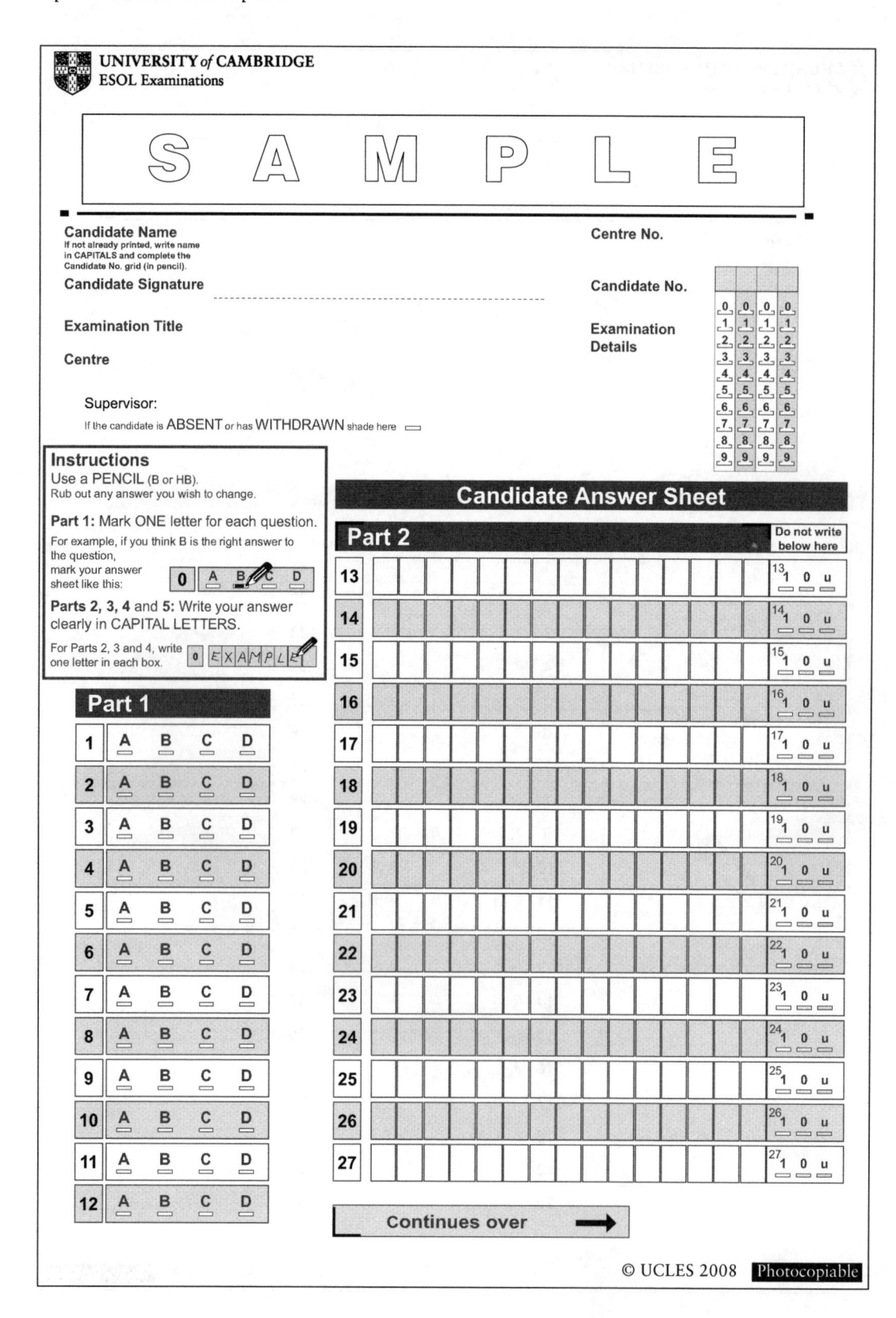

Sample answer sheet: Paper 3

Part 3

	Do not write below here
28	28 1 0 u
29	29 1 0 u
30	30 1 0 u
31	31 1 0 u
32	32 1 0 u
33	33 1 0 u
34	34 1 0 u
35	35 1 0 u
36	36 1 0 u
37	37 1 0 u

Part 4

	Do not write below here
38	38 1 0 u
39	39 1 0 u
40	40 1 0 u
41	41 1 0 u
42	42 1 0 u

Part 5

	Do not write below here
43	43 2 1 0 u
44	44 2 1 0 u
45	45 2 1 0 u
46	46 2 1 0 u
47	47 2 1 0 u
48	48 2 1 0 u
49	49 2 1 0 u
50	50 2 1 0 u

© UCLES 2008 Photocopiable

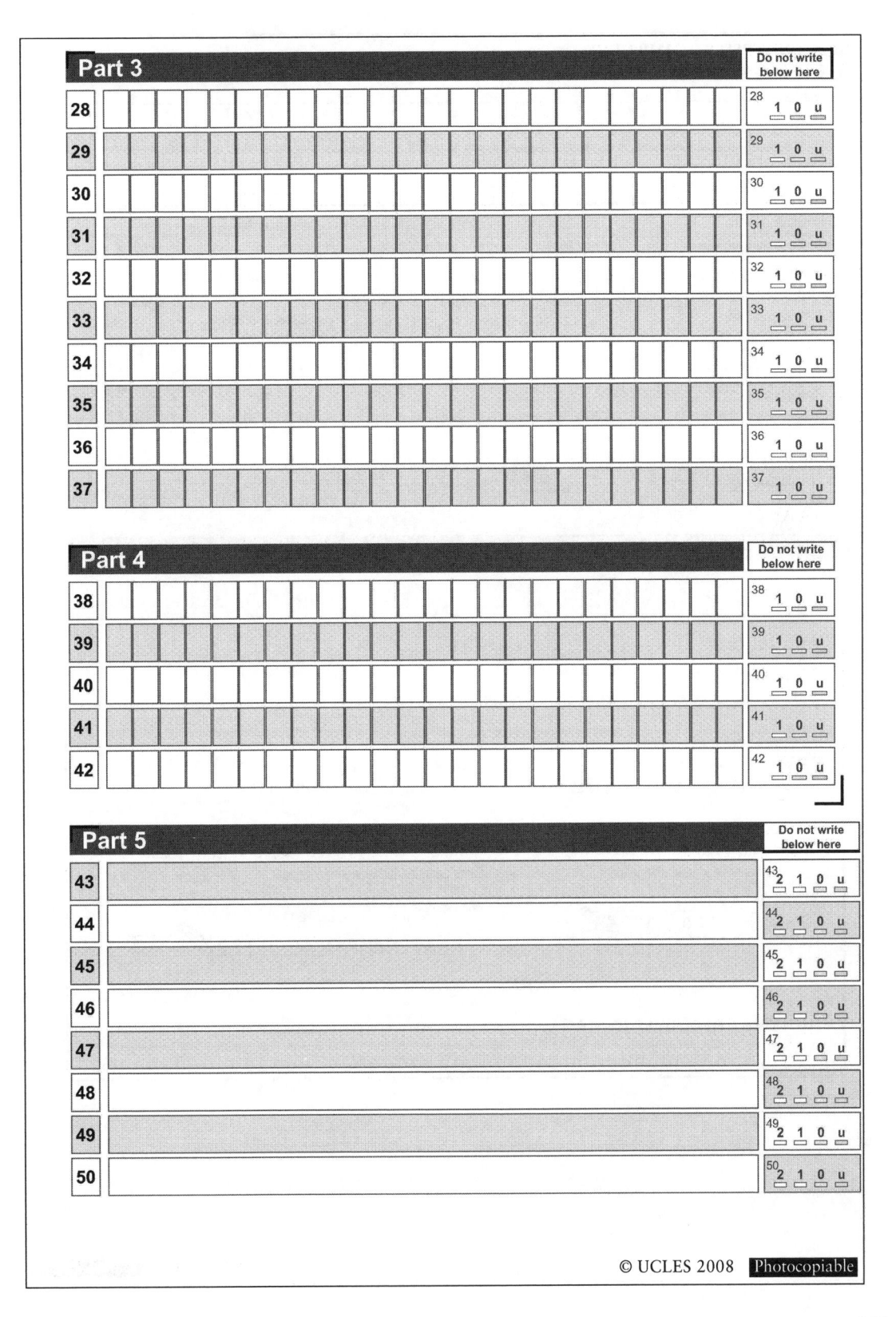

Sample answer sheet: Paper 4

UNIVERSITY of CAMBRIDGE
ESOL Examinations

SAMPLE

Candidate Name
If not already printed, write name in CAPITALS and complete the Candidate No. grid (in pencil).

Candidate Signature

Examination Title

Centre

Supervisor:
If the candidate is ABSENT or has WITHDRAWN shade here ▭

Centre No.

Candidate No.

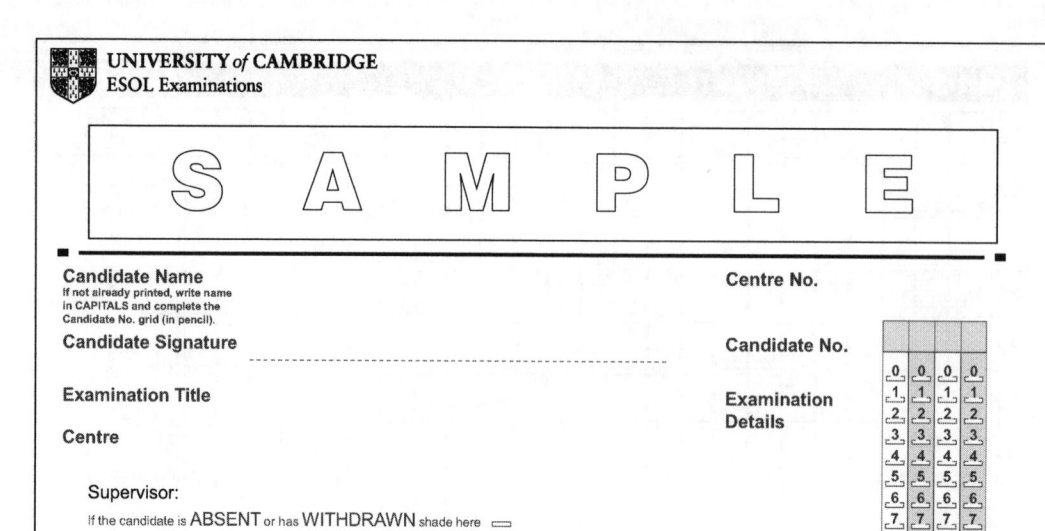

Examination Details

Test version: A B C D E F J K L M N   **Special arrangements:** S H

Candidate Answer Sheet

Instructions

Use a PENCIL (B or HB).
Rub out any answer you wish to change using an eraser.

Parts 1, 3 and 4:
Mark ONE letter for each question.

For example, if you think **B** is the right answer to the question, mark your answer sheet like this:

Part 2:
Write your answer clearly in CAPITAL LETTERS.

Write one letter or number in each box.
If the answer has more than one word, leave one box empty between words.

For example:

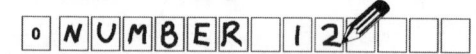

| 0 | N | U | M | B | E | R | | 1 | 2 | | | |

Turn this sheet over to start.

© UCLES 2008   Photocopiable

Sample answer sheet: Paper 4

Part 1
	A	B	C
1			
2			
3			
4			
5			
6			

Part 2 (Remember to write in CAPITAL LETTERS or numbers)

Do not write below here

		Marker
7		1 0 u
8		1 0 u
9		1 0 u
10		1 0 u
11		1 0 u
12		1 0 u
13		1 0 u
14		1 0 u

Part 3
	A	B	C	D
15				
16				
17				
18				
19				
20				

Part 4
	A	B	C	D	E	F	G	H
21								
22								
23								
24								
25								
26								
27								
28								
29								
30								

© UCLES 2008 Photocopiable